Women
in
Television
News

Women
in
Television
News

Judith S. Gelfman

Columbia University Press/New York and London/1976

Library of Congress Cataloging in Publication Data

Gelfman, Judith S
  Women in television news.

  Bibliography
  Includes index.
  1. Women journalists—United States. 2. Television broad-
casting of news—United States. I. Title.
PN4784.W7G4   384.55′4′0922   75-33167
ISBN 0-231-03994-8

To my family—
whose love makes all things possible

preface

Until recently the opportunities for women in television news have been more limited than most of us realized, certainly more limited than I realized until I began looking to work in the field. It was early in 1959, that, with a bachelor's degree, cum laude, from Columbia University and a wide range of professional performing credits in my resume, I was first dissuaded from a career in television news. A CBS executive told me I would never "make it" as a news reporter because I was a "young woman" and he would be "afraid for my safety" on story assignments. He advised me to settle for doing research or commercials. (I did!) A few months later, an NBC news executive suggested that since there is "no future for a woman in broadcasting," I would be better advised to "go home and have babies." (I did!) When I was subsequently offered a job by ABC News, a veteran newsman there warned me of the dire personal consequences to family life of traveling six months or more a year as the assignment demanded. (I didn't!)

Through a study of the careers of women who "did" what "I didn't" and "didn't" do what "I did," I have come to appreciate how often a naïve acceptance of sexual role behavior influenced my own career decisions, and how much unconscious conditioning affected my life-style. Today, I remain convinced that it is possible for a newswoman to produce, intellectually, creatively, and biologically, but preferably in that order. While no one is ever able to do everything in life, a properly timed awareness of alternatives will enable a woman to decide how best to use her talents and energy. It takes exceptional will and courage to know what you are and to become the best of what you can be.

The need continually exists to extend the range of options open to women so that equal professional opportunities become more of a reality. Through a study based on research, interviewing, and observation of newswomen already working in New York television, others will be guided to plan and achieve their career goals within the established limitations. As more women in television news succeed in positions of responsibility and high visibility, the way is paved for those who seek acceptance in traditionally male domains.

acknowledgments

My sincere thanks to the women (and men) in television news broadcasting who gave so freely of their time and made possible the research for this book. I am grateful to them for the opportunity they afforded me to become a close observer of their exciting and demanding profession. The standards they set in their work I have tried to match in mine.

I owe a large debt to Professor Louis Forsdale, Teachers College, Columbia University, who encouraged and supported the idea from its inception as a doctoral dissertation, and to William Bernhardt of the Columbia University Press who helped guide it to final fruition. My thanks to: Professor Paul Kozelka for his many invaluable suggestions; Karen Mitchell for her fine editorial help; the Television Information Office and the Television Bureau of Advertising in New York for access to their library and files.

My deepest gratitude is reserved for my family: my husband, Stanley, who remains my strongest supporter and my greatest source of strength; my daughters, Debra and Sari, who shared so much of my enthusiasm and accepted so patiently the many hours I could not share; and my mother, Rose, whose special prayers on my behalf always mean so much. No expression of my love and thanks could be complete without a memorial to my late father, Samuel Schlein, who is so responsible for what I am and what I do.

contents

That it should be necessary, at this late stage of the human race, to argue that women have a fine and fluent intelligence is surely an eloquent proof of the defective observation, incurable prejudice, and general imbecility of their lords and masters.

H. L. Mencken, 1918

1
breaking ground

Today, more than at any other time in broadcasting history, women are visibly present in the realm of television news. Traditionally, television news broadcasting has been a male occupation. The major news of the world, events that concern men and women equally, has long been assumed to be a masculine perogative. This book focuses on women who are currently challenging that tradition, those women who are now working as television reporters and correspondents on local and network news programs in New York City. It explores the factors which permit women to enter and work effectively in television news and those which deter their full participation. It reveals how some of America's most successful on-air newswomen manage to challenge the mainstream pattern and fulfill the promise of their potential in the predominantly male world of broadcasting.

During the last decade, television has emerged as the primary source of news and information for most Americans.[1] Television has become the medium of communication that is more powerful and more attractive to more people. Ninety-seven percent of the homes in America have a television set, which is turned on for more than six hours each day. Television has become a pervasive aspect of our society. A closer look at television, however, shows that despite its serving all the people, only a small percentage of women serve within it. Of the more than 41,000 persons employed full time in broadcasting in the United States today, 24 percent, or less than one in four, are women. Of these, 89 percent are working in "dead-end clerical jobs." [2] Federal Communications Commissioner Benjamin L. Hooks has warned broadcasters to stop such discrimination against women or face agency action: "Nobody can make me believe that all men are brilliant and smart and innovative and worked hard and that all women were undermotivated and didn't have the ability." [3]

With the single exception of Pauline Frederick, since 1953 NBC's United Nations correspondent, no woman of eminence appeared regularly on network news programs until the 1960s. After the passage of Title VII of the Civil Rights Act of 1964, which makes job discrimination for reasons of sex illegal, a growing group of women reporters began to appear on television news. By 1970 a national survey found that 94.1 percent of the news directors of commercial television stations in the United States said that they would be willing to hire a woman as a reporter.[4] As barriers break down in one area, however,

1 Roper Organization, *What People Think of Television and Other Mass Media 1959–1972* (New York: Television Information Office, 1973), p. 2.

2 Benjamin L. Hooks, "Broadcasters Warned on Sex Discrimination," *New York Times,* September 24, 1973, p. 66.

3 Ibid.

4 Irving E. Fang and Frank W. Gerval, "A Survey of Salaries and Hiring Preferences in Television News," *Journal of Broadcasting,* 15 (Fall, 1971), 430.

Pauline Frederick, NBC News.

they are built up in another. A woman correspondent describes the practice of hiring women newscasters who also happen to be members of racial minorities: "Every station in America feels it must have at least one black and one woman. With a black woman they take care of their tokenism in one fell swoop." [5] Even as opportunities for women slowly strengthen, many prejudicial practices resist change.

In 1971 the Federal Communications Commission (FCC) added women to their equal employment opportunity rule that originally applied only to racial and ethnic minorities. This order prohibits discrimination against women and requires television stations to file affirmative action programs with the FCC outlining their efforts at implementation of equal opportunity for women.[6] As more attention is paid to the dearth of women in the broadcast news profession, pressures mount to increase their participation and to broaden the cultural diversity of the medium.

The first published study of the employment status of minorities and women in the television industry, conducted in 1972 by the Office of Communication of the United Church of Christ, showed conclusively that "television was dominated by white males." [7] Analysis of subsequent findings, while pointing toward positive gains, still reveals a significant imbalance. Numerous television stations fail to comply with the fair employment standards laid down by the FCC, and the agency is continually being pressured to take such employment data into consideration before it grants license renewals. The Reverend Dr. Everett C. Parker, director of the church agency, has stated: "Discrimination against women in both hiring and promotion . . . can be documented in every part of the nation. . . . The

5 Nancy Dickerson, quoted in *Newsweek,* August 30, 1971, p. 62.

6 Federal Communications Commission, *Report and Order.* Docket No. 19269 RM-1722, released December 28, 1971.

7 Ralph M. Jennings and David A. Tillyer, *Television Station Employment Practices: The Status of Minorities and Women* (New York: Office of Communications, United Church of Christ, 1973), p. ii.

right of women to equal treatment with men in hiring, training, promotion and pay needs to be vigorously championed." [8] Correcting inequities through rulings and legislation is only one part of the problem. The greater challenge lies in changing ingrained attitudes and opinions.

For women to be fully integrated into the broadcasting profession, deep-rooted ideas about sexual role behavior must be changed. Powerful systems of belief shape a woman's goals in life and guide her educational and occupational choices. This ideology is transmitted to her implicitly, and is based on a woman's concept of what behavior is appropriate to her female role. The working world is reflective of the world as a whole. The sexes are assigned their respective roles in society: the man is the leader and provider, the woman the supporter. While a man's social status stems from his job, that of a woman, generally, is determined by her husband's position. The female role is centered on the home and being a helpmate. Rarely are purely female activities considered genuinely successful. Since such attitudes are reinforced by our society and are reflected daily on the media, men and women in the professional world tend instinctively to fall into these roles. A woman who cultivates the independence and active striving demanded for successful career attainment defies the conventions of sex-appropriate behavior and often pays the price in anxiety and guilt. Sexism is perhaps best described as the attitude of expectations about women and men, shared by both, that has become an emotional habit. Deep-rooted sexual identity is difficult to change. A psychiatrist on the staff of the Columbia University psychoanalytic clinic has observed that a woman, regardless of her qualifications, "must be twice as good as a man to succeed. She has to combat the prejudice of both sexes." [9]

8 Ibid.

9 Quoted in Lee Graham, "Women Don't Like to Look at Women," *New York Times Magazine,* May 24, 1964, p. 58.

Television news can help effect such change. Television is a powerful force in shaping people's attitudes. When millions of Americans share a common viewing experience, a special significance is added to the function of news. (The "CBS Evening News," with Walter Cronkite, is seen by an estimated twenty million viewers.) [10] When independent and achieving newswomen who have knowledge and stature are seen speaking with authority on major world issues, outdated myths and attitudes are challenged. The image of women on television is elevated and made more realistic. The women who are now successfully working as television correspondents and reporters provide effective role models for others and open doors for those yet to come.

setting. *Women in Television News* looks at a group of women who chose a deviant and demanding career path: the women reporters and correspondents who regularly appear on camera in the presentation of news. The fact that their faces appear regularly before millions of American viewers makes their personal impact important and their achievements more significant. In a visual medium the position of on-air correspondent remains prestigious within the broadcasting industry and in the homes of America.

Since New York is the number one television market in the nation,[11] the city offers the highest competition for success. Most of the newswomen discussed here have achieved recognition through their work on local commercial television stations in New York City. Exceptions are those few prominent women correspondents who currently work at the network

10 Reported by Information Services, CBS News, February 1975.

11 The top ten television markets in descending order of size are: New York, Los Angeles, Chicago, Philadelphia, Boston, Detroit, San Francisco, Cleveland, Washington, D.C., and Pittsburgh. Source: *The Top 25 Programs in the Top 50 Television Markets* (New York: American Research Bureau, 1972).

level out of news bureaus in New York, Washington, D.C., and Chicago.

Statistics indicate a direct correlation between the number of women employed as reporters and both the total news staff and the city size. Women appear with more frequency on television stations located in large cities.[12] New York City is the home of network news operations; consequently, both the quantity and the quality of broadcasters in a New York sample will be high. The factors that allow a woman to succeed in the top New York market should reflect other experiences throughout the country, and the careers of newswomen working in New York can provide insights for others who plan to enter professions where the proportion of women is low and the cultural model remains "males only."

Separate in-depth interviews with 30 women broadcasters provide the basic material for this book. Each interview was designed flexibly to probe for both factual background information and subjective career assessments, based on the perceptions and experiences of women who have achieved prominence in television news. The conflicts and complexities presented by sex-role demands and expectations became more meaningful as each woman disclosed her own background and experiences. The interviews became a process of continual discovery as familiar patterns emerged from the diversity.

The volatile nature of television news made each newswoman elusive, and in many cases months of persistent phoning and follow-up were necessary to set up and complete an interview. At one point, my calls became so repetitious that the person I was attempting to meet told me I was using the technique of Woodward and Bernstein pursuing their Watergate story for the *Washington Post:* "You make so many calls for so long, people begin to feel sorry for you." (I was granted that interview and thereafter made future calls with renewed journalistic pride.)

12 Fang and Gerval, "A Survey of Salaries . . . ," p. 430.

Every woman contacted, with only one exception,[13] was most candid and cooperative and freely gave of her time within the pressured demands of her profession. I was especially gratified by the personal interview time granted to me by those women who have achieved national recognition in television and are among America's most successful broadcasters. Their unique position and range of experiences brought an added depth to the study.

While newsrooms, offices, and apartments were the setting for the majority of interviews, I occasionally found myself taping in more diversified settings: in fancy restaurants and simple cafeterias; in the VIP lounge of Washington National Airport; in the lobby of a Fifth Avenue apartment building in New York (on stake-out for former attorney-general John N. Mitchell); seated in crew cars; and running down the streets of midtown Manhattan.

In three separate cases interviews were conducted over long-distance telephone in order to include all the Washington, D.C., network bureau newswomen (two of whom managed to elude me on my scheduled visit there), as well as a network news correspondent working out of Chicago. Television newswomen appear more frequently on local than on national news programs. Since women network news reporters and correspondents remain rarities (there are only 4 out of 81 at CBS News), their inclusion contributed significantly to the breadth of the book.

The interviews ranged from thirty minutes to two hours in length, depending upon the time demands of the individual newswoman's schedule and her range of pertinent experiences. On-the-scene observations of newswomen in their daily work continued for as long as two weeks with each reporter. The erratic schedule demands of the television news business

---

13 "Personal reasons" were cited by Lucille Rich, WCBS-TV, for her policy of refusing to give interviews to anyone for any purpose. Fortunately, she remained the sole exception.

frequently prohibited my obtaining a block of uninterrupted time. Consequently, field observation and interview often became simultaneous pursuits. This pattern was established at the initial interview and continued for the duration of the research effort.

My first appointment was scheduled with Norma Quarles for 8:30 A.M., January 23, 1973, at her WNBC newsroom office. By 8:40 A.M. I found myself, tape recorder in hand, alongside Norma in the front seat of a crew car headed for a Bronx high school to cover an assigned murder story. Seven hours later, after detailed observation, informal conversation, and copious note-taking, the actual interview was taped in a small restaurant over a belated lunch. The concluding interview took place on August 15, 1973, with Sally Quinn in her CBS network news office just one week after her premiere as co-anchor of the "CBS Morning News." During the intervening seven months, I systematically sought to interview each New York newswoman and to observe her directly at work on actual story assignments. I was on the scene of press conferences, stake-outs, demonstrations, fashion shows, murders, and burglaries, and at hospitals, schools, boycotts, and political confrontations. I was permitted to become an integral part of the working world of television news, often working fifteen hours a day by the side of the indefatigable reporter.

In order to obtain the most relevant and well-rounded perspective of a reporter's role, I also arranged to accompany and observe leading male correspondents in their daily work routine. As I watched some of New York's best known newsmen go through their processes under similar real-world pressures, comparisons became meaningful, and I acquired a greater awareness of the standards for success demanded in broadcasting.

A secondary set of interviews was an important part of the preplanned research. I taped personal interviews with major male news executives and news directors in order to determine their individual assessments, preferences, and experiences concerning television newswomen. The perceptions of these men are valuable, since their decision-making positions give them responsibility for setting institutional policies and for hiring personnel. While many executives were reluctant to speak with me and pointedly refused to cooperate, others freely granted me interview time and full access to their news operations and personnel. The degree of cooperation I received fluctuated greatly from network to network and from station to station, with individual officials often reflecting their respective organizational auras. At ABC the cooperation of management was total and complete. I was afforded ample opportunity to observe every facet of the newsmaking operation, including live studio telecasts of the local "Eyewitness News." Such was not the case at the other networks.

Although I was always concerned with fulfilling the requirements of the research, I was very careful not to permit my presence to become burdensome to management and to their responsibilities of the moment. This was as much good sense as good manners, since much of the research depended on their continuing approval. I began to feel uncomfortable under the scrutiny of WNBC-TV executives when repeated visits to their local newsroom became necessary in order to complete interviews with the selected sample of women (and men). A formal request for additional field observation of local WNBC-TV news reporters was later refused by the news director. At WCBS-TV, the news director requested that I leave the newsroom when he noticed me observing preparations for a sensitive investigative news story. Further access to technical crews and broadcast news personnel was no longer possible. Fortunately, this occurred only after more than six months of participation in all aspects of television news. My research efforts were officially concluded by executive decision. But I had been around newsrooms long enough by then to learn—"that's the way it is. . . ."

2
background
to a career

formal education. For many women in television news, the road to success was a circuitous one paved alternately with blind chance and sacrifice. Considering the backgrounds of these newswomen allows us to determine what distinctive traits and special training motivated or permitted their entry into broadcasting. As a profession, journalism has drawn an increasingly large contingent of women aspirants: in 1971 one-third of the broadcast journalism graduates in the United States were women, compared to 28 percent in 1970 and 15 percent in 1969.[1] Yet the study of journalism in school was not the predominant pattern for our group of women broadcasters, nor does it appear to be the desired one.

All the 30 newswomen mentioned receiving some form of

1 Vernon A. Stone, *Careers in Broadcast News* (New York: Radio-Television News Directors Association, 1972), p. 8.

college training, and 26 (87 percent) hold undergraduate college degrees. Of these, 10 (33.3 percent) received some form of graduate study, including 6 (20 percent) who hold a master's degree or its equivalent. In addition, 3 women attended the Columbia University School of Journalism's summer program for minorities.

The college majors of our group cover a wide academic range. However, the most student interest apparently centered around English, speech, and drama, which together account for one-third of the undergraduate majors (see table 1). Only two women mentioned journalism as their sole college major, while three others cited journalism in combination with another subject. A well-rounded liberal-arts education seems to be the most preferred educational background, according to our group of television newswomen, and is the one they advocate. Several women even felt that journalism school should be avoided. An outspoken example is Ann Medina, former ABC network correspondent, a 1965 graduate of Wellesley College who majored in philosophy and has a Master of Arts degree from the University of Chicago:

table 1. college majors

Major	Number	Percent
Speech and drama	5	16.7
English	5	16.7
English and journalism	2	6.7
Political science	3	10.0
Political science and journalism	1	3.3
Journalism	2	6.7
History	3	10.0
Sociology and psychology	2	6.7
Greek	1	3.3
French	1	3.3
Mathematics	1	3.3
Economics	1	3.3
Philosophy	1	3.3
Physiology	1	3.3
Nursing	1	3.3

Don't go to journalism school. There's been too much emphasis on how to say things rather than on what people are saying. . . . We really, more than at any other time in our history, need people who are experts, who understand this fantastic complex of federal programs, who understand law, who understand economics. We need that more than we need a perfect delivery, or a well-constructed sentence. There are always people who can rewrite your stuff. We don't have the right people who can ask the right questions. . . . Get a graduate degree in economics instead of journalism.[2]

Barbara Walters, co-host of the "Today" show, is the most successful woman in television news today. She is a graduate of Sarah Lawrence College in Bronxville, New York, where she majored in French: "At that time I thought I might teach." Barbara Walters believes that journalism school as academic preparation may be helpful in securing a job in broadcasting:

Journalism school, I think, is like any other master's degree or B.A. degree. If they're studying journalism it is a help and it can be impressive. I think, if someone's hiring you and you went to the Columbia School of Journalism, it's several points in your favor. It's not necessary and it's not the determining factor. . . . You really have to have, I guess, three things: one is the ability to know what makes a story; two is the ability to write it up; three is [the ability] to go out and work with the film crew and put the story together; and four (and it's an intangible quality, it can't be taught) is the ability to deliver it on the air.

2 The quotations are from the taped personal interviews conducted for this study. I am deeply grateful to have been granted permission to use them here.

Pia Lindstrom, WNBC news correspondent, holds a bachelor's degree in history and government from Mills College, Oakland, California. She studied acting in London and had several bit parts in movies before beginning her television career. Pia states her recommendation succinctly:

> I'd get a job. I wouldn't waste time getting a degree in journalism. I'd get a job on your local or university paper. That's the place to begin. Get experience reporting and learn how to write a story and how to be a reporter and how to mix with people.

Interviews with the male executives in the broadcasting profession who in fact are responsible for most of the hiring that is done presented a divided preference. Six (40 percent) of our group of 15 men expressed a distinct preference for a journalistic background. Kenneth A. MacQueen, Vice-President and General Manager of WABC-TV, states: "Journalistic formal training is not required, but it would be an asset."

One-third of the men were not interested in any particular college degree but preferred, instead, a broad range of experience. Av Westin, Executive Producer, ABC News, declares: "We have some correspondents who are not college graduates but they've had enough broad experience to fill in that gap." An NBC News Vice-President curtly comments: "I've seen fine reporters never get out of high school."

The remaining four male news executives opted for a liberal-arts background for their news reporters. Of this last group, a News Director who is himself a product of journalism school and a journalistic family, reflects on his preference anonymously:

> I'm still not convinced that a journalism school can teach anybody anything they can't learn in six months as a copyboy. I can remember being at Syra-

cuse and being told that one of my credits for journalism was learning to recognize 160 type faces.
Now, at the *Herald Tribune* . . . we had six type
faces. They fill your head with trivia. . . . Political
science, the social sciences, literature, a basic
grounding of the tools you use, I think, is far more
important than the technical training you get at journalism school.

These findings support an earlier study of the educational
preferences of news directors in the United States in which the
majority favored hiring a reporter with two years' experience
and no college education.[3] Without experience, these same
news directors preferred a college graduate in broadcast journalism rather than a college graduate with another major.

While both the women and the men whom I interviewed
emphasized the importance of experience, a basic foundation
in the liberal arts was the educational background chosen and
approved by the majority. Journalism school was not considered a necessary prerequisite for success in the profession, although many male executives remain favorably impressed with
such formal training.

family background. The family backgrounds of
our group of television newswomen are quite varied and in
their diversity represent a wide range of socioeconomic characteristics. The majority of the women (56.6 percent) were born
in the northeastern part of the United States, with 7 originating
from New York City. Of the others, 5 came originally from the
Middle and Far West; 3 from the South; and 4 were born outside the United States.

All but 7 newswomen (5 from New York and 2 from Wash-

3 Irving E. Fang and Frank W. Gerval, "A Survey of Salaries and Hiring Preferences in Television News," *Journal of Broadcasting,* 15 (Fall 1971), 431.

ington, D.C.) left their home towns because of job transfer and career advancement. Geographic mobility remains a recurring factor in the career climb of the women (and men) in broadcasting, with New York City remaining the number one television market in the nation and, consequently, a focal point for success within the profession.

An analysis of these newswomen according to placement within the family shows that 13 (43.5 percent) were the youngest child in families of two, three, five, and six siblings. There were 6 among the group who were the only child and another 6 who were the eldest child in their families. The remaining 5 were born as a middle child with two or four additional siblings.

Neither the number of children within the individual family structure nor particular placement at birth seems to have influenced the career choice or attainment of the newswomen. Where there are other female siblings in a family, most are reported in noncareer roles. No single person, family relation or otherwise, was singled out as being influential in the choice of broadcasting as a profession. Each woman was the only person of her family to enter television news. It is said that the best way to get a job in television is to have a relative in the business. These newswomen did not.

An analysis of the women by father's occupation shows that 15 (50 percent) of them had fathers who were businessmen, either salaried or managerial; 8 were engaged in professional occupations; 4 were blue collar workers; and 3 worked for the government. Not one woman singled out her father's occupation for role-model identification or direction.

Among these television newswomen, whether a mother worked had little perceptible impact on her daughter's career development. One third of the group had mothers who had never worked. For the rest, most mothers worked only occasionally at times before or after the birth of their children. With singular exceptions, the newswomen recalled that economic considerations prompted their mothers' work decisions; personal fulfillment was a secondary consideration. For most of the group, the mother's employment was viewed in terms of a "job" and not a "career." It is difficult to determine what kind of role model each mother offered for her daughter, since success for a woman in our society can be achieved within the confines of her home. Negative as well as positive images remain with these newswomen from their mothers' work experiences and from their early upbringing.

Gloria Rojas, WABC-TV correspondent, recalls that her mother "worked on and off in hospitals. It's obvious you don't mop floors and empty bed pans because you want to be fulfilled."

Sylvia Chase, CBS News, relates that she was raised by foster parents. Her real mother held "various jobs" for economic reasons:

> She was not an aggressive feminist. My grandmother was a suffragette. . . . I was raised to believe a woman could do anything that a man could do. . . . I was stunned at first and I guess I've never really accepted the idea that a woman can't do whatever the hell it is she wants.

Pia Lindstrom did not enjoy her early career attempts at acting because people were always quick to compare her to her famous mother. However, as a successful television correspondent, Pia has established a separate identity which she says has enabled her to become something other than "Ingrid Bergman's daughter."

Not one of the women I spoke with showed any reluctance to break with familial patterns and values. Although readily identifying their parents' religion (40 percent were Protestant), most women maintained that they had no religious affiliation or were nonpracticing. If these childhood family variables exerted any influence on the newswomen in this group, it was more through the subtle factors of social conditioning rather than through overt teachings. Each one was imbued by her family with a positive attitude toward productive work. Their inheritance is perhaps best viewed as an intellectual curiosity, an independent spirit, and a capacity for growth.

first jobs after college. The choice of a broadcasting career was neither direct nor immediate for most of our television newswomen. Documentation of their various career paths proves them to be as diversified as the group of women traveling them. This may be, in part, due to the differing cultural demands for men and women in our society regarding preparation for a career. The fact that a man will be gainfully employed for one-third of his adult life is an established premise on which his life plans are based. For men, society creates no basic need for a choice as to whether or not to work. For women, however, society first demands that a basic career decision not interfere with her expected family role.[4] This severely restricts her range of choice and her work pattern. It is her success as a wife and mother that is the criterion for judgment of a woman's ability in our culture, not her career commitment and independence. Such sex-role conditioning has been a significant factor in discouraging females (and males) from developing their full human potential.

This is documented by the experiences of Trish Reilly, WCBS-TV correspondent, who was graduated in 1964 from the University of California with a B.A. in English and "with no career goals whatsoever." Trish relates:

> I'm the oldest daughter and his [her father's] great dream was that I would be a school teacher,

4 Lotte Bailyn, "Notes on the Role of Choice in the Psychology of Professional Women," in Robert J. Lifton, ed., *The Woman in America* (Boston: Beacon Press, 1967), p. 238.

right? In that era you were very contemptuous of the idea that one went to college to learn a trade. . . . You were there to develop your mind. . . . I believed I could step into a nice job some place. . . . The first thing that anyone says to you when you go to apply for a job is, "What's your typing speed?" and "Can you take shorthand?" neither of which I could do. So I spent a year and a half just drifting. I was Gal Friday to some lawyers and then Gal Friday in a real estate firm. . . . I spent a year as a stewardess and I don't regret it. I traveled all over the world. I quit after one year and came to New York. . . . I had friends who had been researchers at *Newsweek* magazine and they had said it was a good deal. . . . I was the ideal woman to go to work as the *Newsweek* researcher because I didn't perceive myself as a bright girl who was capable of doing anything. I had a very low self-esteem, very low self-confidence. I was just a pretty face in a miniskirt, which was what they wanted at *Newsweek* magazine. . . . That was their whole image of women. They were completely contemptuous of the intellectual ability of a woman.

An analysis of the first jobs held by the newswomen after leaving college shows that only 8, or 26.6 percent, worked in some capacity in television at the outset of their professional lives. Among the wide range of jobs held by the remaining women, teaching was most frequently mentioned, with 5 initially making a start in that direction; 4 began by writing for newspapers or magazines, and 3 others first attempted an acting career (see table 2).

Of the 8 women who went directly from college into the world of television, not one found a warm greeting extended to her. For a few the interest in broadcasting was always there. For the others the conscious commitment came through gradual evolution and even happenstance. But once in television,

table 2. first job after college

Job Category	Number	Percent
Television (any phase)	8	26.6
Teacher	5	16.7
Writer (newspapers and magazines)	4	13.3
Actress	3	10.0
Secretary, Gal Friday	3	10.0
Social worker	2	6.7
Nurse	1	3.3
Speech pathologist	1	3.3
Research assistant	1	3.3
Assistant buyer	1	3.3
Stock broker	1	3.3

whether on the threshold or well beyond the doorway, each woman worked long and hard to remain inside.

Marlene Sanders, ABC News, attended Ohio State University and Cleveland College, where she majored in speech. She describes her professional start in a "flunkey-type job" as a production assistant, "a go-for" on Mike Wallace's show on Channel 5, WNEW-TV, in the mid-fifties: "I'm a fast learner. The more I learned, the more I wanted to move along . . . I was lucky to get that first job. . . . Luck, break, and circumstance often determine direction." Marlene Sanders was later to become the first woman to anchor a network evening newscast: "I broke the ice and the networks didn't collapse." She was the first woman correspondent to be sent to Vietnam: "I've never been in a situation where being a woman has really been a problem."

Rebecca Bell, NBC News, a graduate of Cornell University with a major in English, intended to go to law school but did not have the money. She got her first job on station WDSU-TV, an NBC affiliate in New Orleans, by "making the rounds." She was hired basically as a "Hey, you" and describes being paid half of what a man was paid because, she was told, "you're a single woman and you have no family and you shouldn't need very much." Her salary level changed only when the American

Federation of Television and Radio Artists (AFTRA)[5] came in and said, "either pay her full scale or fire her." Rebecca recalls that her boss "came very close to firing me."

Maureen Bunyan, CBS News, graduated in 1968 from the University of Wisconsin and decided to try to get a job with a local television station in Milwaukee: "At first they said no, but I persisted. . . . I had quite a few problems with the station in getting a job, based on the fact that I'm black. . . . I was very determined that that was not going to get in my way." Maureen came to New York in the summer of 1970 to enroll in the Columbia University School of Journalism's minorities program.

The factors affecting the choice of a first job are complex enough without the added burden of racial and sex-role discrimination. Such considerations are an integral part of hiring practices in all professions, and certainly become critical criteria in the highly visible broadcasting arena. Often, race and sex can be used to advantage at key times in the job market. More often they can not.

By their second job after college, 63.5 percent of the sample had begun to work in some area of television. For some of the women several months was sufficient time to suggest the need for a new job. For others a decade passed before a new career was attempted. At the point of their initial entry into the television profession, the majority of the women were filling jobs as secretaries, trainees, production assistants, and researchers. Two began by working in educational broadcasting and one started by doing a television program for children.

By the third job change, 87 percent of the women had found their way into broadcasting. Of the 4 who still remained in another job category, when they finally did make their move into television news, 1 arrived from newspaper reporting and the 3 others from radio reporting.

Pat Collins, WCBS-TV News, received a Bachelor of Science

5 The American Federation of Television and Radio Artists is the labor union governing on-air television performers.

degree in 1963 from Simmons College in Boston, with majors in journalism and political science. She spent less than a year in Mexico "doing sort of social work" before going to Los Angeles to work for "a small, terribly right-wing newspaper, *The San Gabriel Valley.*" This experience was beneficial mainly because on her return to Boston, "I could look the managing editor of one of the Boston newspapers square in the eye and when he asked me, Have you worked on a newspaper? I could say, I certainly have!"

Pat worked for the Hearst paper in Boston for the next 3 years, first doing "woman's drudge," and then after several months "convinced them I could do hard news features." Her television start "was flukey." A newspaper strike in Boston resulted in the educational television station there asking "a group of us to do a newspaper of the air at night. . . . We just talked about the stories we would have written about had there been a newspaper." This initial television exposure led to a daily "3-hour live magazine show" called "Panorama" on WTTG-TV in Washington, D.C. She co-hosted the show "with 2 other men, naturally. . . . Guess who did the fashions?"

In 1968, after doing this show for over a year, Pat got an offer to go to San Francisco "to do my own show. That was an ego massage, and I was too young to know any better. I didn't have an agent, I didn't have a lawyer and when I think about it now, I was really very naïve." The program was called "Hotline," a talk show that took phone calls from the audience: Pat says, "The talk show taught me a great deal personally, so I don't regret that. I do regret it professionally, but personally I don't regret it."

She then moved back to Boston to work for WBZ-TV, the NBC affiliate station, as a film and theater critic. Her reviews were done for the 11:00 o'clock news, and since few people were really doing film and theater criticism in those days, Pat feels it was "like so many things, we'll let *her* do it, the throwaway." She soon began to do the weekend news "with a man" in addition to her reviews. Consumer news also became her assignment, and she looks back to this time as "the best experience of all, I suppose, those three years in Boston."

Pat Collins made her move into New York television when she accepted a job with WNBC-TV news: "I have a friend who says if there is no reason to stay, go—and there were no overriding reasons to stay. I had done all I was going to do at that station" (WBZ-TV). In the fall of 1974, after 2 years as a "street reporter" for WNBC-TV, Pat became the hostess of her own program, the "Pat Collins Show," which appears daily over WCBS-TV. She is also that station's arts editor and reviews films and theater for the 6:00 and 11:00 o'clock news.

Interviews with all the women indicate that perseverance, hard work, proper timing, and luck contributed to their rise within the television profession. For some it was years of struggle before advancement was possible; for others advancement took little time and less effort. Fifty percent of the women arrived at their present positions as on-air newscasters after frequent vertical and lateral changes within the broadcasting hierarchy. Six took advantage of minority training programs in their career climb, while 3 used radio reporting as their stepping-stone. Only 5 of the women entered their present positions without any prior broadcasting experience or affiliation. Of these, 4 came into television news reporting with writing experience on a newspaper, a magazine, or a wire service (see table 3).

The fifth, Rose Ann Scamardella, WABC-TV news correspondent, is a 1968 graduate of Marymount College in Manhattan, where her major was sociology. She received her master's degree in sociology from New York University by going at night: "Sociology helps a New York City reporter understand people. This is important in human-interest stories." Rose Ann first worked for two years as a registered stockbroker and then spent another two years working for a shipping company in personnel management. While there, she was appointed to a

table 3. career chronology

Name	Position (at time of interview)	Previous TV Job(s) (affiliation)
Rebecca Bell	NBC network correspondent, Chicago	Reporter (WMAQ; WRC; WTOP; WKYC-TV; WDSU-TV)
Theresa Brown	WPIX-TV reporter	Reporter (KYW News Radio, Philadelphia)
Maureen Bunyan	WCBS-TV reporter	Reporter (WGBH-TV)
Sylvia Chase	CBS network reporter, New York	Producer (KNX News Radio)
Connie Chung	CBS network reporter, Washington, D.C.	Reporter-writer (WTTG-TV)
Pat Collins	WNBC-TV reporter	Film and theater critic (WBZ-TV); Co-host "Panorama" (WTTG-TV)
Pauline Frederick	NBC United Nations correspondent	ABC News (free lance)
Phyllis Haynes	WOR-TV Co-host "Straight Talk"	Reporter (WPIX-TV)
Carol Jenkins	WNBC-TV reporter	Reporter (ABC); Reporter (WOR-TV); Co-host "Straight Talk" (WOR-TV); secretary (CBS)
Pia Lindstrom	WNBC-TV correspondent	Reporter (WCBS-TV; KGO-TV)
Catherine Mackin	NBC network correspondent, Washington, D.C.	Reporter (WRC)
Marya McLaughlin	CBS network correspondent, Washington, D.C.	Reporter (CBS network, Washington, D.C.); associate producer (CBS); secretary-researcher (NBC)
Mary Helen McPhillips	WOR-TV reporter	Reporter (WOR Radio); commercials, news (CBC Toronto)
Marjorie Margolies	WNBC-TV reporter	Reporter (WCLU-TV
Ann Medina	ABC network correspondent, New York	Reporter (WKYC-TV)
Sara Pentz	WNEW-TV reporter	Reporter (WBNS-TV)
Norma Quarles	WNBC-TV reporter	Reporter (WKYC-TV)

Name	Position (at time of interview)	Previous TV Job(s) (affiliation)
Sally Quinn	CBS network co-anchor "CBS Morning News"	Reporter (Washington Post)
Trish Reilly	WCBS-TV correspondent	Writer (Newsweek Magazine)
Gloria Rojas	WNEW-TV co-host "Midday"	Reporter (WCBS-TV)
Betty Rollin	NBC network correspondent, New York	Theater critic (NBC-TV)
Marlene Sanders	ABC documentary producer and correspondent	Assistant Director of News (WNEW); writer-producer (WNEW-TV)
Rose Ann Scamardella	WABC-TV correspondent	Personnel manager (American Export Industries)
Linda Shen	WNBC-TV reporter	Associate Producer (WNET); writer and Associate Producer (WNEW-TV)
Lynn Sherr	WCBS-TV reporter	Writer (Associated Press)
Virginia Sherwood	ABC network correspondent, Washington, D.C.	Reporter (WKBS-TV); co-producer and on-air hostess (WWL-TV)
Lesley Stahl	CBS network reporter, Washington, D.C.	Reporter (WHDH-TV); research-writer (NBC-TV)
Judy Thomas	WOR-TV reporter	Production assistant (WGBH-TV)
Melba Tolliver	WABC-TV correspondent	Secretary (WABC-TV)
Barbara Walters	NBC co-host "Today"	Writer (CBS); producer (WPIX); Assistant Director of Publicity (NBC)

nonsalaried position as a Commissioner of Human Rights for the City of New York, deciding discrimination cases. Her plan was to go to law school full time, but two days before she left her job, an ABC producer interviewed her for possible inclusion in a profile series on women: "They were thinking of doing a profile on me because I was only 24 and a commissioner."

The next week she received a call from Al Primo, then WABC-TV News Director: "He told me he wanted to talk to me about a job offer. . . . I auditioned and the following week I was on the air. I just came out of nowhere."

While success in television news broadcasting apparently required varying gradations of effort and experience from the women in our group, many divergent paths merged as individual career courses were charted. All the women, bright, articulate, and ambitious, were ready to seize an opportunity and advance with it. While a few women created their own opportunities, many others profited from opportunities that were created for them.

Barbara Walters is considered the "queen of television news." A recent survey found her to be the best known and most popular personality on American television before lunch. In our interview she recalls her start in the professional world:

> It didn't seem to me that I had any great talent. I liked to write, and at one time I had wanted to be an actress, but I knew that I never had the push for that. I had a lot of pull but no push. . . . I came to NBC and went to the personnel department. My father had been very well known in show business then [6] and I didn't want to capitalize on his name. And the personnel department told me I had no show-business background and I should go to secretarial school. So I did. So I got a job as a terrible secretary in a small advertising agency. And then there was an opening on the local station here as the Assistant Director of Publicity. And I knew all the columnists at that time, which meant that my boss went out and had lunches and went to Toots Shorr's and I sat and did all of the

6 Her father, Lou Walters, was a theatrical entrepreneur and vaudeville booking agent who started a nightclub called The Latin Quarter, first in Boston and then in Miami and New York.

Barbara Walters, NBC, co-host "Today."

releases. . . . And then in a little while I was made a producer. At that time I was the youngest female producer. . . . I was then out of school two or three years, and I learned a great deal then working on the local level. . . . I began to produce local shows at NBC—entertainment shows and interview shows. I left NBC to work for WPIX to produce a woman's show. . . . Finally, I went to work at CBS. . . . I went to the news and public affairs department working on the early morning shows which were designed to knock the "Today" program off the air. . . . I worked on a show that starred, if you can believe it, Dick Van Dyke and Walter Cronkite and it was a flop. So names don't make it and neither one of them were [then] very big names. Somebody had faith in both of them. Cronkite did the news and Van Dyke did songs and chatter. . . . And I worked on various shows and they all went off the air. Each show always had to have one female writer. They would fire the whole staff, hire a new producer, and he would hire me as the one female writer. . . . I then went to work for a public relations firm. . . . I hated public relations but I learned a great deal because it was my job to take our clients and get them on radio and television. Among the clients was, I remember, a housebuilder in Long Island, and it was he who had the model kitchen at the fair in Moscow that Nixon and Khrushchev had their meeting in. . . . I always wanted to be on the "Today" program, but they always had one female writer. These writers were unionized. You couldn't fire them. You couldn't and still can't. And the only way that there would be an opening would be if the writer left, and it was a very good job and she wasn't about to leave. Finally, I was hired by a man who had been a producer at CBS, [the late] Fred

Freed, who is a documentary producer, to write and produce five-minute inserts into the program. We don't have them now, but we did then. They would sell five minutes to a particular sponsor, who in this case was Green Stamps. Green Stamps hired Anita Colby. She did little mini-interviews and I wrote them for her, and that's how I got hired. . . . One day the new producer of the program (also from CBS) who is also a documentary producer, a man named Shad Northshield, said, "Barbara can write anything the men can write," and I then did. I wrote whatever stories came up, and it remains the same today. . . . So that when the time came that the last person who was on the program, who was an actress, did not work out, and it was still the time when what one did was to hire an actress or an actor, . . . I was already on the air enough so the audience knew [me] and I was accepted in somewhat of an authoritative way. I continued my first year to go out and do those filmed stories, and do today when I have the time. . . . If I didn't have to work at one point to support myself—I had a lot of dingy jobs I didn't like—I would have stopped. I mean, the way most women stop. I would have got married or had babies or let Daddy support me. Most men can't do this. They go through all the dreary jobs and so eventually they make it. . . . Too many young women, and I think this is a fault of women's liberation, feel they're going to start in at whatever it is interests them. They don't want to do all the grubby work.

Sally Quinn wanted to be an actress when she was graduated from Smith College in 1963 with a drama major: "I had been discovered by an MGM talent scout at Smith in my senior play and he wanted me to go on television. But that didn't work out. . . . I imagine I wasn't that dedicated that I wanted to starve." She then took on a variety of research and secretarial jobs in Washington, D.C., Mexico, Europe, and New York:

> These were all at least two months long. . . . During the 1968 campaign I worked for Eugene McCarthy and for Robert Kennedy. . . . Then I became secretarial assistant to Richard Salant, who is the president of CBS news. And he took me with him to the conventions in Miami and Chicago, which is how I got to know everybody at CBS. . . . I went back to Washington and got a job at the Institute for Policy Studies and did that for several months. Then I went to California and came back. It was then that I was called by the *Washington Post* and asked if I wanted to be a reporter. . . . I knew social Washington very well because my parents were involved in it—political, diplomatic, social Washington.[7] . . . They just thought it would be good to have someone who knew social Washington and could perhaps hopefully learn to write. It was an experiment. . . . So I was hired personally by Ben Bradlee, who is the editor of the *Washington Post,* and I began working as a reporter.

Exactly four years later Sally Quinn was hired away from the *Washington Post* to become co-anchor of the CBS "Morning News":

> They wanted someone who could write. They wanted a woman journalist. . . . I think one of the reasons may be because Barbara Walters was on the "Today" show and that Barbara Walters has been

7 Her father, Lt. General William W. Quinn, was until 1965 Commanding General of the Seventh Army. He is now retired.

very effective and very good. . . . They knew me, you see, because I had worked as Mr. Salant's secretary. . . . And they followed my career. . . . They interviewed other people and I made a pilot and they liked it. . . . My whole professional career in journalism has been such a freak. I mean, who ever got a job at the *Washington Post* without ever having written a word? Who ever got a job as a co-anchor on a network television broadcast who has never been on television before? It just doesn't happen. . . . It has just come to me. It's fallen in my lap. I haven't gone out after it and I don't know what I would have done if I'd been starting out.

Pauline Frederick, NBC News, the dean of women journalists, majored in political science at the American University in Washington "when it was very new and very young." There was no journalism course, so she decided on a law career and received a scholarship at American University, where she earned a master's degree in international law. Her advisor then told her, "since Washington has so many lawyers, you'd better go back into journalism." Pauline Frederick describes her early efforts to enter the broadcasting profession:

I tried every way I could to convince the powers that be that I could broadcast news. . . . This was very difficult because it was unheard of for a woman to want to enter this man's world. . . . I remember asking an executive (not at NBC) what I could do really to get an opportunity to broadcast news. I didn't want to go out and cover fashion shows, as they were having me do. . . . He said, "When you are broadcasting something as serious as news about the United Nations (this, of course, was only radio; it was a long time ago), listeners are going to tune out

. . . because a woman's voice does not carry authority." And I always follow up this anecdote with the
comment that I am terribly sorry I didn't have
courage enough in those days to tell him that I knew
his wife's voice carried plenty of authority in his
house. . . . I guess I was just stubborn. I'm not a
suffragette. I don't think women should have positions just because they're women. But I do resent
discrimination, and I suddenly realized that I was
being discriminated against just because I wore
skirts. (In those days pants could not be worn in the
office.) So consequently this made me determined
that, come what may, I was going to break that barrier.

She remembers being told about "directives from higher up"
not to use her on air, unless she got "exclusive stories":

So from that time on I really worked very hard to
try to get exclusive stories from the UN way out in
Flushing and Lake Success, thereby having the
chance to get on air more than otherwise. . . . The
times were just not right for women to move into this
area. . . . There was discrimination against women,
certainly, and it was very difficult for, shall I say, the
male world to accept a woman doing hard news. . . .
I was somewhat of a curiosity because I was the only
woman broadcasting news.

Lesley Stahl, CBS News, was graduated cum laude in 1963
from Wheaton College for women in Norton, Massachusetts.
She did postgraduate work in zoology at Columbia University
"because I wanted to be a doctor." She changed her mind
"when I married a doctor." She then went to work as the assistant to the Director of the Technical Division of the Population

Council: "I didn't enjoy it at all. I thought they were keeping me down because I was a woman." She answered a *New York Times* advertisement and became an assistant to Mayor Lindsay's speechwriter: "I decided I wanted to be a television reporter while I was working for Lindsay." So she applied to CBS and NBC at the time when they were gearing up their election units:

> I went right to the head of the election unit [at NBC] and he hired me. I did not go through the personnel office. I was savvy enough at that time to know that was not the way to get a job. . . . It was absolutely just lucky timing for me. Then the "Huntley-Brinkley Report" hired me and sent me to London. . . . It was a lateral movement. I had the same title, researcher-writer. . . . I quit after eight months because I was doing nothing. . . . It was a dead end. And, in fact, Dick Wald, who is now the President of NBC News,[8] told me at that time that I never was going to make it from the top, the top being the network level. And that if I was really serious—which they all doubted, thinking I was a flighty blonde or a dilettante—if I ever was going to make it, I was going to have to start from the bottom. And I was going to have to prove myself by going on a newspaper staff, or going to a local station, or working for one of the wires. . . . He was the first and only person at NBC who was really ever honest with me. . . . It was very painful to hear because I thought I was going to be able to make it within NBC, and he told me right out I wasn't. David Brinkley, by the way, told me that I never was going to make it. And I want to tell you that was a great incentive in my career. . . . I didn't

8 Richard Wald was then a vice-president of NBC News. Reuven Frank was the President of NBC News.

take the remark from Dick Wald . . . to be a sexist remark. . . . I didn't think David Brinkley's remark was a sexist remark either at the time. I don't even in retrospect. I just think he was judging me saying in his head I was a dilettante and wasn't going to make it. I don't think a man would look at a man and say, "You're a dilettante," though. I think it's a natural thing for a man to say about a female.

After two years on WHDH, a local television station in Boston, Lesley Stahl went to work at the CBS network bureau in Washington, D.C., as a general-assignment reporter:

It was a coming home. It's what I always wanted to do. . . . Friends of mine tell me that when I worked for Lindsay I used to say all the time, what I'm going to be one day is a reporter on the "Walter Cronkite Show." . . . When these particular people first saw me on CBS, they called and said, "I've never known anybody who has gotten what they've really always wanted."

Sara Pentz, former WNEW-TV reporter, is a 1959 graduate of Ohio State University, where she majored in English and journalism. She got her first job on a local CBS affiliate, WBNS-TV in Columbus, Ohio: "I badgered them to death and they finally hired me as kind of a nothing in their news department there." She left this job to come to New York City "because that was my ultimate goal. I wanted to get into television, and it wasn't easy. I was desperately looking for a job at this point." A job opened up at *TV Guide* magazine as picture editor, and she spent the next four years there and then two more years as an associate editor of the *Saturday Evening Post* until the magazine folded:

I job-hunted for ten months, which is an agoniz-
ing experience. It's the loneliest time of your life. But
I organized myself and presented job-hunting as if it
were in fact a job, which is what everyone must do if
you are in this business job-hunting. . . . I had eighty
interviews during that period, and eighty interviews
is a lot of interviews. And then I was very lucky. . . .
In June 1969, I read a two-inch article in the *New
York Times* saying all stations in the local area were
going to be covering the space shot. "Ah ha!" I said.
"They're going to need extra help." So I wrote letters
to all the local stations saying, "I'm yours. I'm available. Anything you want me to do. I can write, I can
organize. I can do a little film editing, whatever you
want." So Channel 5 called me up and they offered
me the choice between two weeks with the space
shot or a job as a vacation replacement writer. And I
took the vacation replacement writer.

In the fall of 1969 there was no more room in the budget for
her job as a writer, so Sara Pentz asked Ted Kavenau, then
news director, to give her a chance as a reporter. She was told
to come in every day from 9 to 6 and dream up story ideas and
then to come in weekends as a writer:

On my first day I turned in fourteen story ideas;
the second twelve, and Ted said, "If you come up
with something really good you can go out and cover
it yourself." Well then, for the next three months I
worked seven days a week, about twelve or so hours
a day, probably more, and I would do everything and
anything. . . . I worked Christmas and New Year's
and the whole thing. Early in January, Penny Wilson,
their female reporter, left, and Ted called and said,

"Congratulations, you have just been made our female reporter."

Melba Tolliver, WABC-TV correspondent, graduated in 1959 from the Bellevue School of Nursing of New York University and practiced nursing for a year and a half on the staff of Bellevue as an operating-room nurse. She started working as a secretary to the network operations manager at ABC in October 1966:

> I took the job with the idea that I wanted to work in television news. I thought at the time I wanted to be a researcher, but there weren't very many people that I could go to for any real firsthand information on qualifications to become a researcher—what the job was like, what the pay was, etc. So after searching around for a while for somebody to give me advice, I figured the best thing for me to do was to just get a job with the news organization and find out for myself. So I said, well, six months and I'll have some idea what's involved. . . . About five months after I was here, there was the AFTRA strike. The man I worked for at the time was part of the committee of people to work up contingency plans. . . . In their contingency plans they assigned a man to a five-minute network news show, "News with the Woman's Touch," to replace Marlene Sanders. When the strike happened, the sponsors, from what I remember, didn't want to have a man doing that program. So there was a big last-minute search through the company for a woman to do that. . . . There weren't very many women at that time, so the search couldn't take very long, and they didn't get anybody. So my boss asked if I would substitute, if I would just sit in and read the copy for that show just that day.

Melba Tolliver, WABC-TV "Eyewitness News."

. . . It was just a lark as far as I was concerned. And I did substitute and they didn't get anybody else for the duration of the strike and I continued. And there was a lot of publicity because it was the first strike in the history of AFTRA. For the writing press it was a different kind of story, all these people coming from jobs that had nothing to do with on-the-air work replacing people: the man who replaced Walter Cronkite, another fellow who did weather, and me. And so there were lots of stories about us. After the strike ended, ABC decided to set up a training program and I was the trainee. . . . It was, I suppose, this station's reaction to the Kerner Commission Report about the lack of minorities in all areas of the news. They didn't have any real program. I was fortunate in that instance in that I could sort of set up my own program, and I did; that included working at ABC and rotating through the various departments of the news, so that I got at least some idea of the working of the various departments. Then I also went back to NYU and took some classes in writing and reporting, and that really has been the extent of my formal education in journalism. . . . So much of what I have learned about journalism has been from on-the-job experience and observing other people. The training program lasted about eighteen months. . . . There was another strike in September of '67. . . . This time it was the engineers, but AFTRA people went out and I again substituted for Marlene Sanders.[9] . . . This time it wasn't a lark. I was uncomfortable because I was strike-breaking, and because I didn't want to get up there and make a fool of myself. . . .

9 Both women assert that Marlene Sanders has never spoken to Melba Tolliver because of her failure to support the strike action.

And then in July 1968, I was hired as a full-time general-assignment reporter for this station.

The interviews reveal that women correspondents are drawn from a diversified range of backgrounds and that their career paths exhibit an equally variegated design. The major portion of our group acquired their most useful knowledge while working as journalists and not through formal educational plans. It is often stated with practical wisdom that the best diploma comes from the "graduate school of hard knocks." But regardless of capacity and training, access to the television profession was easy for some and difficult for others. The constants that emerge are strong spirit, acquired competence, and an increasing determination to attain professional recognition in broadcasting.

3
career dimensions and expectations

age. Physical characteristics play no small part in the ability of television newswomen to fulfill the norms of the broadcasting profession. The structure of television news bears directly on a woman's acceptance in the field and her ability to remain a full, practicing member of the television news world. The median age of the newswomen in our group is 34 years. There is a span of forty years between the youngest woman and the eldest. Fifteen (50 percent) of the women were in their thirties at the time they were interviewed for this study; 9 (30 percent) were in their twenties; and 5 (16.7 percent) were in the forty-year range. There was only one woman who has remained in the television news profession past the age of 45. Pauline Frederick, for the past twenty years NBC News United Nations correspondent and the only reporter ever ranked among the ten most admired women in the world by a Gallup poll, met with me just one week before her mandatory retirement.[1] As she sat in her office in the press section of the Secretariat building overlooking the East River, she quietly told me: "I have reached the retirement age. So it's about time for me to lock up the desk and move on." The poignancy of her momentary hesitation following these words remains fixed in my mind as a fitting description of "the eloquence of silence."

There is, apparently, a double standard of aging in the world of television news, with the older woman finding herself a victim of media neglect. Elinor Guggenheimer, Commissioner of Consumer Affairs under Mayor Abraham D. Beame and former co-host of "Straight Talk" on WOR-TV,[2] speaks with characteristic candor of this problem:

> Prejudice against women, you see, is many, many times intensified against older women. You are viewed not as an intellect but as a body. Don't kid yourself. With all that women have done to fight that kind of concept! Astonishingly, even women's liberation has paid extraordinarily little attention to the older woman and to the fact that her job is limited because she is [older]. They say that women shouldn't be sex objects, but you damned well better be a sex object if you want to get ahead in television.

Trish Reilly was hired as a television correspondent by WCBS-TV at the age of 30. At her audition she was advised by a woman correspondent already working at the station:

> Look, if you're going for a correspondent's job and you're going for an on-camera job, you have to

1 Pauline Frederick plans to lecture and to write in her retirement. NBC has appointed Richard Hunt as her successor at the United Nations.

2 Elinor Guggenheimer is 62 years young. She outran me, my tape recorder, and Broadway traffic during the course of our interview.

go now. They will not hire women at 26 because they're too young to look credible. They're still pretty young things. On the other hand, you can't come back again when you're 35 and say you want the job because you're too old. So if you want to make the move, they hire at age 30, and that's when you have to do it.

Trish Reilly herself comments on the need for women to remain forever young on camera:

> I don't see why it's essential that a woman has to look thirty-ish whereas Walter Cronkite can look sixty-ish. . . . I think it could be a terrific boon to women if they could see news presented by women who are in their own age bracket—in their forties, in their fifties—and still see that these women are valuable to society.

If advancing years presents an obstacle to a woman's acceptance in television news and prevents the existence of a middle-age image, appearing too youthful may also be a problem. The youngest newscaster in our group, Linda Shen, was dismissed by WNBC-TV after working there for seven months as a summer replacement. She was then 23 years old:

> I feel that my three major handicaps have been (1) I'm a female; (2) I'm Chinese, and (3) I'm young. If I really thought about it, maybe it's my youth that's working most against me.

More than three-quarters of our newswomen were hired for on-air work while in their late twenties or early thirties. It presently appears that the job of television newscaster belongs to the 30-year-old woman. As the young women who are now working successfully in television news grow in experience and in maturity, the American audience should be able to view the reality of women growing older as they do the men who remain broadcasting through the years. Marlene Sanders, 43, recently remarked on the inability of women to grow older on television: "That's too bad. I think I've gotten a lot smarter lately!" [3]

salary. Television broadcasters are well paid for their endeavors. Over 90 percent of the television newswomen I interviewed are presently earning salaries of more than $20,000 a year from their on-air television work (see table 4). More than one-third of the women receive a yearly income of more than $30,000. Only two correspondents made over $51,000 annually,

table 4. yearly salary

Salary	Number	Percent
$11,000–$20,000	2	6.7
$21,000–$30,000	14	46.6
$31,000–$40,000	9	30.0
$41,000–$50,000	0	0.0
$51,000 and above	2	6.7
No answer	3	10.0

while another two made less than $20,000 each year. These figures become more meaningful when compared to the statistics from the United States Department of Commerce, Bureau of the Census, in which the average salary of a female college graduate working full time in 1971 was $9,162. On the other hand, male college graduates earned an average annual income of $14,351.[4]

Salaries are determined by a base pay scale set by the American Federation of Television and Radio Artists, the gov-

3 New York Times, September 28, 1974, p. 18.

4 U.S. Department of Commerce, Bureau of the Census, We the American Women (Washington, D.C.: U.S. Government Printing Office, 1973), p. 8.

erning labor union of all on-camera performers. Added to this base salary are a declining scale of performance fees for each live television appearance and overtime pay. Personal contracts are held by many women correspondents which include a larger base salary and no individual fees. These contracts, negotiated by the woman herself or by her business agent, are usually dependent upon her experience and how great a demand exists for her services. On-camera news broadcasters are regarded as "talent" by management, and in all monetary negotiations viewer appeal is a prime consideration.

Rebecca Bell explains, "You are referred to as a piece of talent, and that's what you are. You are contracted for and bought and sold." At one point in her news career, Rebecca tells how Westinghouse Broadcasting wanted a director who was under contract to NBC and NBC "wanted me—so they traded bodies."

Pat Collins, one of the three women I interviewed who refused to reveal her yearly income, remarked: "If you're valuable to the station, if they need you, then they pay you." Melba Tolliver concurs: "In this kind of job, people are paid not just because of their ability, or their facility as a reporter, but they're also paid because of their value in helping to build an audience and attracting people to watch this station."

Only three women in the group felt that a salary differential due to sex existed in their profession. Union scale regulation was the factor overwhelmingly cited as responsible for equality in pay. Management officials were in complete agreement concerning the absence of any income differential between men and women working in television news.

In opposition to this view is Phyllis Haynes, of "Straight Talk," who appears daily on WOR-TV. She states:

> Equality in pay does exist for male and female reporters in most cases. It is the area of anchormen and executive producers that is almost void of

women. Consequently the high-paying, decision-making positions still go to men with only a few exceptions. There are extremely qualified women in both network and local operations capable of anchoring, running entire news operations, and handling all management decisions. Only when these areas are shared with experienced women broadcast journalists will we be able to say that there is no income differential between men and women.

Barbara Walters is the most economically successful woman in the television news world and the only one in our group to earn a salary above $100,000 annually. At the time of our interview, Barbara Walters was in the midst of negotiating a new contract that reportedly gave her a substantial increase in income. She is said to earn nearly $400,000 a year now from her work both on the "Today" show and on her syndicated program "Not For Women Only," which she proudly told me is "the highest rated show in its time period" in New York. On the question of salary differential due to sex, Barbara Walters commented: "I get paid more than many men working here but less than a man in a comparable position."

Our interviews lead to the conclusion that pay inequities for most women working on air in television news broadcasting are minimal. There are presently many more male correspondents than women earning salaries above $50,000. This can be attributed to the lack of opportunities for women in former years to enter broadcasting. The leading news anchormen command salaries in excess of $100,000 and $200,000. Tom Snyder, WNBC-TV's early evening anchorman reportedly earns $420,000 a year for his various network assignments, including his work on the nightly "Tomorrow" show. These 6-figure salaries are justifiable in the economics of television. The audience appeal of the television anchorman is considered the key to the rating success of the entire newscast. The identification with the anchorperson is the single most compelling reason given for viewer preference. An increase of a single rating point in the New York market is considered to be worth half a million dollars in additional revenues for the station. Women, new to the profession, are not the "proven winners" demanded by rating-hungry executives. It is interesting to note, however, that after twenty years of distinguished service, Pauline Frederick's income from television news was in the same range as the incomes of many women who were on the job for less than a year.

physical appearance. All the newswomen I interviewed readily acknowledged the importance of physical appearance in their profession. Their individual attractiveness attests to the need for better-than-average looks in the world of television. Among this group of women working in television news are those who, on camera or off, would be regarded as "beautiful." Their photogenic qualities, however, differ by degrees, with certain faces treated more kindly through the camera eye than others. Nonetheless, they are an extraordinarily good-looking group of women. Melba Tolliver speaks emphatically of the importance of good looks for on-camera television success:

> Have you ever seen a really ugly person on television, who might have been the most brilliant person in the world? We'll never know because we haven't seen it. . . . I think now you're beginning to see some variations from the stereotyped blonde, or blue-eyed white male, or brunette male. And now you're seeing people with hooked noses, black skins, long hair, mustaches. . . . Television is so imitative. If somebody has a Puerto Rican reporter and proves to be successful, then other stations do the same

thing. Somebody makes a little headway and then they say, "Well, it's all right, so now we'll go in." I had a lot of difficulty with this station when I started wearing my hair in an Afro. It was in June of '71. I was taken off the air for a while because that's how unrealistic they can be at times about what's going on in the real world. I mean, they could see people on their game shows, women, wearing Afros, and yet they couldn't accept that in their own news department. So appearance is very important, and television is just as much in the business of perpetuating images as its advertisers are.

Many of the newswomen shared with Maureen Bunyan the belief that "image" is of prime importance to women:

A woman is always expected to present a more positive physical image of herself than a man is under all circumstances. A woman is defined by society by the way she dresses, looks, speaks, behaves. A woman who is in public a lot is forced to be conscious of those things because other people force her. . . . I think of myself as a reporter trying to do a specific job which ought not to reflect on the way I look, and vice versa. However, because the medium in which I work is television, I know the visual is important. I cannot tell a story to an audience with my hair in curlers. They wouldn't listen to me. I cannot tell a story dressed in some outlandish costume because I will not be accepted. So the goal basically is an accepted physical image.

The "accepted" image in television appears to have undergone change through the years. Rebecca Bell thinks that in this respect television is getting better:

You don't have to be a beauty any more, but if you're obese or you've got a bad case of acne, forget it. They just won't put you on. You've got to be just generally acceptable.

Virginia Sherwood also feels the difference in image represents a positive gain for the industry:

> I think we're coming into an age in this country where people are beginning to be more natural, and networks, businesses, are letting people be what they are, and women be women, without trying to shape them into a sex-symbol or a non-sex-symbol or an anything. So the news is important and not your looks. . . . I think all those rules have loosened up to whatever is easiest and natural, providing you keep an image which is you, but a good, clean image.

Marlene Sanders reflects on the changing emphasis in physical appearance:

> Women who were on the air in the early stages always had to be better looking than comparable men. The men who do the news are not particularly gorgeous and I'm not saying all the women are. But they tend to be better-than-average looking. This is because women, I think, have always been judged partly by their looks, and looks have been excessively important. I think this is diminishing a little bit, that some of the women now on the air are more on the average side. And that's fine, because it shouldn't be the consideration that it always has been. I think if you're doing news you want to appear a serious person, and you don't want to look like a

> *Playboy* bunny. You don't want to look like a society
> woman. You want to look like Brenda Starr . . . cas-
> ual, straightforward, not phoney.

The problems involving personal appearance most often
mentioned by the newswomen related to hair style. Marjorie
Margolies wore a wig at one point in her career rather than cut
her long black hair: "At one point a boss asked me to cut my
hair, so I wore a wig for a while. When he left I took the wig off.
He just thought I looked better." The need to smile was another
troublesome issue for many women. Barbara Walters says: "I
don't smile enough on the air. I try to smile a little if I do think
of it." Marya McLaughlin retorts to people who suggest she
smile more, "I don't see a lot of smiling men." Pat Collins finds
it difficult to smile when you deal with serious subjects: "You
can't joke around about an explosion in Staten Island." Un-
derlying the concern about on-camera smiles is the need expressed by many newswomen to soften their on-air delivery
and visage. Ann Medina criticizes herself for being "a little too
hard." She explains the problem: "A lot of women are much
too hard on the air. We shouldn't be soft, little feminine
women. But we can be more natural, a little realer."

Eyeglasses were a frequent point of contention for performing newswomen. Pauline Frederick states that years ago there
was "some desire on the part of executives that I wear contact
lenses instead of glasses. . . . As far as glasses are concerned,
if I see better with glasses I wear glasses. If I see better with
contact lenses, I see with them." Lesley Stahl is the only television newswoman who regularly appears on camera wearing
glasses:

> My glasses have been one of the biggest debates
> of my life. . . . One day my mother called me
> up—and it was recently—and she said, "Forty-nine

Lesley Stahl, CBS News.

million Americans saw you on television tonight. One of them is the father of my future grandchild, but he's never going to call you because you wore your glasses."

The cosmetic problem of glasses extends into the male domain as well. Walter Cronkite began to wear contact lenses on camera after he received a letter suggesting it from Abbie Hoffman. Hoffman now states:

I get a special thrill these days watching the news 'cause every time I look deep into Walter's eyes and catch the slight reflection of his contacts as he turns to Eric Sevareid . . . I know that in some small way

> I've helped create him. Just as in some way he's helped to create me.[5]

Management was less ready to admit to the existing emphasis on physical appearance within the broadcasting profession. William Sheehan, now President of ABC News, states:

> I can't think of anybody that was turned down because he or she didn't live up to some standard of appearance. I think your question implies something about age or beauty or handsomeness and that's not one of the criteria at all.

Av Westin, Executive Producer, ABC News, says:

> I don't care what they look like. The only dress code we had is that the correspondent should not be dressed more casually than the person they're interviewing.

Robert Mulholland, NBC Television News Executive Vice-President, believes the sole criterion is that physical appearance must not detract from the story:

> We have all sorts of people in terms of physical appearance. The only thing that we look for is people who are not making an editorial statement with their physical appearance, because that gets in the way of a story.

Al Ittleson, Vice-President, ABC News, believes the key to the success of "Eyewitness News" is definable:

5 Abbie Hoffman, "The Eyes of Cronkite," *Esquire*, April 1973, p. 85.

> Our people come across as real people. They're not all beautiful. They're not all handsome. They don't speak English that well. They are regular, average-looking, average-sounding people, and I think that's the key to anyone we hire here.

He candidly admits to the importance of physical appearance on television:

> It's unusual to see an unpleasant looking person on television. It's important because the first impression is a physical impression. . . . Bill Ryan . . . [is] a fantastic reporter, really good, but he always had to be secondary because he wasn't as handsome as Jim Jensen or Bill Beutel or Roger Grimsby. . . . Women have a further burden. Women are supposed to be beautiful. People anticipate what a woman is supposed to look like, so when they come to television—I haven't seen an unattractive woman on television yet. So they have even a greater burden. In fact, they're hired, I would say, probably hired more because of the way they look and their image than because of their background. A man with a very strong journalism background and a man who has broken stories . . . can get away with a little bit of homeliness. Men aren't expected to always be attractive. Women have a tougher time.

One outspoken news director expresses his views anonymously:

> You cast a news show and you quite definitely want four or five people that are different. There isn't a quota system. . . . I haven't gone as far as the ex-

ecutive who once sent out and said, "I need a Chinese American with an Italian surname, female."

. . . You want five interesting looking people, and a great deal of the appeal of a news show is the interaction of their personalities. "Eyewitness [News]" proves this beautifully. Roger [Grimsby] can interact with anybody including Atilla the Hun. He's beautiful at it. I don't have that kind of talent. All my people are very straight still. I try to loosen them up. That's the influence of the Walter Cronkite old iron-bottom school of journalism. Getting people to loosen up is quite difficult.

Ted Kavenau, former Vice-President and News Director of WNEW-TV, realistically admits the need for a distinct personality in television:

This is a mass medium and you want people with a mass appeal. . . . Compare Gabe Pressman, for instance, with Roger Grimsby: two totally different types, but each one has its place. You can be successful with almost any kind of guy. It's almost unpredictable.

It is this intangible, unpredictable element that makes television executives continually seek new personalities. Stations are constantly working at changing the style, appearance, and format of their local newscasts in the perennial battle for viewer attention. The news process becomes exploited in the attempt to deliver a large audience to sponsors. Edward R. Murrow, considered to be one of the finest journalists television has produced, said the basic problem is that television news "has grown up as an incompatible combination of show business, advertising, and news. . . . I am frightened by the imbalance, the constant striving to reach the largest possible audience for everything."

Images are carefully chosen and perpetuated. The need is for a person with "presence"; someone the audience will be eager to watch, thereby increasing the ratings and revenues of the news programs. Just such an indefinable quality allows individual correspondents to become "stars." This permits the distinction between the television news business and show business to blur.

The inability to divide show business and news is evident in the stress on the "anchorman" of the evening network news programs. The emphasis on image permits competence in journalism to become secondary to cosmetic qualities and an ability to maintain high ratings. One news executive told me caustically: "TV tends to hire people who *look* like they know what they're saying." No one is exempt from the ratings race. The able and talented Walter Cronkite, very much the boss of the "CBS Evening News" went into oblivion for a time when the increased ratings of the rival NBC Huntley-Brinkley team caused panic and fruitless experimentation at CBS.

It is precisely such capriciousness that causes the fear and insecurity that permeate the halls of the television world and are reflected in the daily lives of all whose jobs are at the mercy of mass audience acceptance.

Chris Borgen, WCBS-TV correspondent, is a dedicated television newsman who spends 80 percent of his time "on investigative reporting. There are very few of us around." Chris believes that "early in this game it's necessary to decide whether you're a television personality working as a journalist or a journalist working in television." Chris leaves little doubt of his own preference:

> I'm in the television end of the news business. Most of the others are in the news end of television. . . . I'm a journalist first who happens to be working

in television. I'm not a pretty face, obviously. I couldn't care if I look like Dracula on that tube if I'm presenting the facts to the people.

Daily exposure before millions of Americans results in the broadcasters' becoming superstars and public personalities. The problems presented by the celebrity-journalist factor were dramatized when WABC-TV correspondent Geraldo Rivera was rebuked for violating ABC policy and publicly endorsing the 1972 presidential candidacy of Senator George McGovern. ABC stressed that the newsman is a celebrity by virtue of his association with the news operation, and that any endorsement involves the entire news organization; a political endorsement also affects the credibility and independent judgment of the journalist in the mind of the viewer. Geraldo Rivera, a winner of several broadcasting awards, maintained that the entire thrust of the "Eyewitness News" format is to make its newspeople into personalities, and that he has "never made any pretence to objectivity." [6]

Martin Berman, Geraldo Rivera's producer at WABC-TV, described the crusading, personal approach Geraldo brings to the news: "All of Geraldo's journalism is personal. Those who agree with Geraldo are the ones who like him." The reaction of the average person in the street to the physical presence of Geraldo is impressive. While I worked on assignments with him, requests for his autograph were commonplace. One particular young woman, upon receiving her paper signed "To Janet—Love and Peace, Geraldo Rivera," reacted with supressed hysteria: "I think I'm going to die!" I came to understand why Geraldo has stated with unreserved pride that "Everyone in New York knows my face, and if they don't know my face, they've heard my name."

If no one image completely prevails on the television news

6 Quoted in John J. O'Connor, "The Geraldo Rivera Case and the Rights of TV Newsmen to Speak their Minds in Public," *New York Times,* October 23, 1972, p. 64.

screen, also no single physical attribute or manner is permitted to interfere with the main job of the news correspondent, which first and last remains communication. Most of the women broadcasters described their on-air manner in terms of naturalness, honesty, sincerity, accuracy, directness, and "believability." Pauline Frederick outlines a camera technique used by many women in their television work today:

> I try to speak as simply and directly as I can into the camera because when I began broadcasting many years ago, I was told by a news director who was very wise, I thought, . . . that what he wanted me to do was to cover a story and then come back and tell it as though I were narrating it to a member of my family or to a friend. . . . in other words, talk it, and I have tried to keep that in mind through the years.

Currently, the informal, relaxed delivery is in vogue. The successful ratings of WABC-TV's "Eyewitness News" program have inspired a new trend toward individuality and spontaneity in manner. Traditional journalists are encouraged to add touches of humor to their reporting. Conversational banter is encouraged as the reporter seeks to relate to the story. Speech coaches are hired for many on-air news correspondents to improve voice, delivery, and personal style. In this contemporary trend of reporting, "looseness" is a carefully calculated effect. While pomposity is a bore, on camera or off, frivolity is equally offensive in the television newsroom. Hopefully, audiences will respond favorably to news programs that operate effectively at the "television end of the news business."

assignments. Television news, both on the local and on the network level, relies mainly on the general-assignment news reporter or correspondent—that is, each broadcaster is expected to cover any number of subjects with relative facility. The emphasis on the generalist rather than the specialist permits the most efficient use of available personnel. Pat Collins spoke for most of our newswomen when she described her daily assignments while a "street reporter" as "a little bit of everything. . . . Except for sports and weather, there are few specialists here. We don't have enough people to go around."

Most news reporters average three stories each day. Those who work for the smaller independent stations are often given four different news stories to cover. Judy Thomas, who is sent out to cover "everything" at WOR-TV, states: "We have to work fast because we are a small station and we don't have much money and we don't have many crews."

Whether covering one story or four, each local news reporter repeats a similar work pattern. Lynn Sherr described her daily routine while a reporter with WCBS-TV:

> Normally you go out and shoot your film on the same day as you use it. I come in at 9:00 or 10:00, depending on what my hours are. I'll get an assignment—be somewhere by 10:00 or 11:00—and go out with a film crew; come back by 1:00 or 2:00. The film goes in to be developed; you start talking to the associate producer and figure out how you're going to put the piece together. The film comes out of the soup; you go back into film editing; screen the film; figure out how you're going to structure it; go and write the script; go back with the film editor, putting it all together. By then it's 4:30 or 5:00 o'clock, if you're lucky; go and write live open or close; 5:30 you get made-up and 6:00 o'clock you're on the set. . . . The producer decides who is on set live. It's a question of how many bodies they want on the set; how many bodies they'd rather have on film. You ask before leaving, "Do you want me on the set or do you

want me to do a film close?" Sometimes the 11:00 o'clock producer will ask for a film close, although I go live on 6:00 o'clock, so he can recut it and use it on the 11:00 o'clock show . . . . I sometimes go 14 or 15 hours a day. And you have to look nice, of course, which takes even more energy.

On general assignment, Lynn was also expected to "cover everything":

You must be able to switch gears very quickly. You've got to be able to think very quickly and organize very quickly, so when you're thrown into a situation you don't understand, you can pick out the important elements quickly and efficiently and tie it into a decent package.

Lynn Sherr admitted an assignment preference: "I like doing stories on women if I can do them in a way I think is contemporary. Women have a whole new way of thinking about themselves and people have a new way of thinking about women, and I think it's important to report that."

Even those women news reporters with an expressed interest in a special area are expected and assigned to cover every kind of available story. Marjorie Margolies considers her specialty "children, adoption, abuse, and foster care." The WNBC assignment desk will give her these stories whenever possible. She has sponsored and adopted Leeheh, an 11-year-old Korean girl, and was in the process of adopting a Vietnamese child: "It's my thing. I really don't know how to explain it. It's what I want to do with my life. I will adopt and give homes to as many kids as I can." In this case, story preference and personal lifestyle reinforce each other.

Sylvia Chase, hired as a general-assignment reporter for CBS network news in New York, feels a responsibility to find and suggest stories of her own:

I'm not particularly interested in doing spot news.
I do it perfectly well, but I'm much more interested in
doing depth stories, and I have sort of carved out a
specialty for myself in the woman's field. I don't think
we do enough of that kind of news. . . . I am interested in the woman's movement as a story. I think it's
one of the best stories we've got around. It's a story
that we systematically ignore—not intentionally. I just
think it's hard for men and for a hell of a lot of
women to understand this thing—how important it is,
how basic it is, and that it is insidious. It is in every
single American home, and I don't care if the woman
wants to be barefoot and pregnant all the time. She's
feeling the pressure.

Since many newswomen are sensitive to the need for more
women to cover hard news stories without, as Marie Torre says,
"the unpardonable discrimination against my sex that relegates
women in TV news to feature trivia," [7] they react negatively to
certain kinds of assignments. Barbara Walters explains:

One of the things that I think is a little sad is that
women who in the last few years have been trying so
hard to be recognized as reporters have in many
cases refused to do any sort of female features. So
that a good deal of the lighter side of the news and
some of the humorous and anecdotal side of it is
now being taken over by the men. But this will pass, I
think. . . . There are some women, like Liz Trotta,[8]
for example, who refuse to do any story that has to
do with women. I don't feel that way. I like stories
that have to do with women as much as stories that

7 Marie Torre, *Don't Quote Me* (Garden City, N.Y.: Doubleday, 1965), p. 224.

8 Liz Trotta was NBC network correspondent stationed in Singapore during the
period of my research. She has recently been reassigned to New York.

Marjorie Margolies, WNBC-TV "Newscenter 4."

have to do with men. But I do think that we have to prove ourselves in the straight news story.

Sara Pentz, formerly the only woman reporter at WNEW-TV, was sent out, at first, on whatever story was available. She was assigned a lot of crime stories "and so I became the crime reporter around here. If there was a fire, I covered it." She was then made the society editor in an effort by management to "liven up the news show." Her assignments became attempts "to sprinkle the show with a little bit of gaiety." While believing there is a place for this kind of story in news, she was not really happy doing society features: "There is no controversy or guts to it, and I like controversy."

Pauline Frederick is a veteran of the United Nations. She is unique in her specialty: "My responsibility is to cover the United Nations in all aspects that might make news." She chose the United Nations as her specialty "because this was the center of international activity, and since I had always been concerned with international relations, this seemed to be the one place . . . toward which I gravitated all the time."

Washington bureau news reporters and correspondents have a specialized range of assignments because of the nature of the nation's capital. Marya McLaughlin is a general-assignment CBS news correspondent but she covers "mainly the Hill and mainly the Senate." Lesley Stahl is a CBS network correspondent in Washington who made an impact with her Watergate coverage. She said in our May 1973 interview:

> I just cover Watergate. . . . I started going out with Bob Woodward of the *Washington Post,* whom I met when I was covering the Watergate story. He said, "You've got to make a story your own story. That's the only way cub reporters ever make it. Stick like a barnacle to it." . . . I'm so numb and I'm working so hard and I'm so involved. It's so time consuming,

thoroughly engrossing, all my energy goes to my job. Everything goes to it, and I'm worried about it. But, you know, you speak to Bob Woodward and he's one of the two reporters who dug up this whole story. He's in the same position. It has nothing to do with men-women. It has to do with involvement in a story.

Virginia Sherwood worked for five years as a general-assignment correspondent with ABC news assigned to the Washington bureau:

> I'm responsible for anything that they give me, any kind of story. . . . I guess my favorite thing about news is people. And I'd rather do people stories than thing stories. . . . I did the first in-depth interview ever done with the [former] first lady, "A Visit with the First Lady." Mrs. Nixon and I did that well over a year ago. This was the first time she had ever done anything on TV. . . . I thought there was a Mrs. Nixon that nobody had seen and, of course, that definitely emerged in the last year or so. . . . I happen to be right now going to do a profile story on Lindy Boggs, who undoubtedly will be our next Congresswoman from Louisiana. Her husband, as you recall, was killed in Alaska. . . .[9]

There is a definite distinction between local and network news assignments. Network news is all national or international in scope. Since there are very few women working at the network level, those who hold these positions gain additional prestige and the opportunity to travel all over the world. Rebecca Bell, NBC network news correspondent in the Chicago bureau, pinpoints the difference:

9 On Tuesday, March 20, 1973, ABC television news aired the story of Lindy Boggs after she won a special election to fill her husband's congressional seat.

> Eight years of local television after a while gets a bit repetitious and dull. . . . After a while it just seems like the same story with a different dateline. . . . With the network, because there are so few of us that are correspondents, you don't cover cities, you don't cover districts, you cover the nation, you cover the world. I went to Russia with Nixon, Iran, Poland. . . .

As a result, network correspondents are constantly traveling. Rebecca Bell relates that while covering the national election campaigns: "I left Chicago in February and except to run in a couple of days here and there to pick up fresh clothing, I didn't come back to Chicago until November 10th." Betty Rollin tells of her first assignment as an NBC network correspondent based in New York:

> The first week I was sent to Arkansas. Then it just happened that there was a murder in Missouri and I was the nearest person to the murder, so I was sent to that. So I wound up working around the clock for three or four days and then the following week I did nothing for a couple of days.

It is interesting to note that while the distinction between reporter and correspondent often connotes increased prestige, salary, and experience on the part of the latter, this is not always the case. After ten years of experience as a general-assignment reporter for various local stations, Rebecca Bell was promoted to network correspondent at NBC in February 1973:

> I was told by several executives, "Forget it, you'll never be a correspondent. Why don't you go into management. Why don't you do something else." . . . I trained some of the men that they named cor-

Rebecca Bell, NBC News.

respondents. [Who can be] a correspondent is a personal judgment. There are so few of them. They decide what person on the air can carry believability. . . . They didn't feel people would want to see me as a network correspondent.

Betty Rollin was made an NBC network correspondent in January 1973, with one year of broadcasting experience:

I was hardly ready to be a network news correspondent. . . . Someone, I suppose the president of news,[10] felt that I, because of my writing and journalistic background, would ultimately work out as a cor-

10 Richard C. Wald is the President of NBC News.

> respondent, although I didn't have the technical
> know-how. . . . Whoever had that belief, I think, felt
> it was worth taking a chance on me.

Betty Rollin's appointment as a correspondent at NBC
prompted this comment from another woman correspondent at
another network:

> That caused quite a bit of unhappiness, which is
> nothing personal against Betty Rollin. But quite
> often, people will want to be correspondents and will
> be told, "No, you're good and we like you, but you
> haven't got the necessary experience." Well, that
> whole theory, that whole response is completely un-
> dermined when they bring in Betty Rollin, who
> from all I've heard is extremely bright, extremely
> pleasant to work with, but she doesn't know how to
> do it yet. And the network level should not be, had
> not been used in the past as a training ground for
> correspondents. Women are being discriminated in
> favor of here. She has a presence on the air that
> some people say is more important for a woman than
> for a man. A man would never be hired who hadn't
> had the experience, just purely because he had great
> presence on the air.

Long and erratic work hours are a common characteristic of
the news profession. News correspondents at local and network offices often work fourteen hours a day, with weekend assignments rotated on a regular basis. Night shifts are a
frequent necessity. In May 1965, when Marya McLaughlin became the only women reporter on the CBS network staff, she
was assigned to work the news desk in New York. For the first
six to eight weeks, Marya was assigned the 8:00 to 4:00 shift,
and then she worked the overnight, midnight to 8:00 shift for a
year:

I never learned to live with that. . . . There was a girl who was running the traffic desk, and there was a woman who was on the overnight for radio as a producer, and my desk assistant was a woman. So when the world came to an end, we took over.

Early morning live news programs require the most unusual time demands. When Sally Quinn went on air live at 8:00 A.M. each morning, she followed a unique time table:

I get up at 1:17 [A.M.]. . . . I figured it out. I need thirteen minutes to wash my face, brush my teeth, and throw on my clothes. . . . I don't have to do anything to my hair or makeup because that happens here. So I always look like a wreck when I come in. . . . I go to bed at 6:00.

Norma Quarles arrives at the WNBC-TV newsrooms at 5:30 A.M. each day in order to prepare for the 7:25 A.M. news show, but she enjoys it: "There are no bosses early in the morning. I make all of my own decisions. There's no hassle. . . . I've worked every schedule in the day, I guess, and I like this early one best."

Most correspondents consider themselves on call twenty-four hours a day, seven days a week. Since the news profession reacts to what is happening in the world, individuals have little control over their time and work schedules. Betsy Aaron, ABC News, considers news broadcasting to be the most time-consuming of all careers:

It's one of the most demanding job fields I can think of. . . . The biggest man in this business, I guess, is Walter Cronkite, and Walter Cronkite's time is not his own. . . . No matter how big you are in this business, you have no control.

satisfactions of job. The biggest reward for the professional news reporter has been described as "a ringside seat at the best show on earth." Our newswomen single out the satisfaction of being present as history is happening and being part of the most crucial stories of the decade. Rebecca Bell recalls the most meaningful moments of her career:

> There are feelings that stick out. I think being part of history—like standing in the White House press room when Kissinger came out and announced peace in Vietnam. Or landing with the White House press corps in the Moscow airport, and the American flag and the Russian flag were flying together.

To Phyllis Haynes, the satisfaction comes from "the exposure to other people who are shaping the future of the country, who are shaping the future of the world." For Ann Medina, the gratification remains "the dream of reaching someone with a new idea."

Several women found the most rewarding elements of their on-camera television job involved the power they are able to exert to help people and to initiate change. Gloria Rojas explains:

> Most rewarding is when you feel you've made a difference. I made a difference once, an important difference. There was a woman on Medicaid and there were Medicaid cuts. She had oxygen delivered. With Medicaid cuts she could no longer pay for the oxygen and she couldn't live without oxygen. She was going to die. So I collected money at CBS when I did the story to keep her oxygen going, and I went down to the Department of Social Services, who took up their own personal collection to remedy the situation.

Often career satisfaction stems from unexpected headline statements uttered during an interview. Barbara Walters recalls some particularly memorable interviews in a television career distinguished by important interviews:

> Certain hard-to-get interviews—an interview with H. R. Haldeman a year ago when really no one knew who he was. The only interview he's ever done on television and he made what was a headline statement that those who disagreed with the president's peace plan were aiding and abetting the enemy. . . . And the ones that still give me the most personal satisfaction are the stories of the handicapped children. Those are the stories that change your life, not the celebrity ones. . . .

Marya McLaughlin remembers most fondly her interview with Martha Mitchell at her apartment in the Watergate:

> I went down and went in, and there was a producer and a film crew, and I said, "Is there any particular reason that we're doing this?" . . . She was a new cabinet wife and they said, "No, you may talk about anything." And it was at that interview that she made her statements about sending all the demonstrators to Russia and caused all that storm. I just couldn't believe it. I just kept staring at her and smiling and the interview kept going on. And I just said, "Well, what do you think of William Fulbright?" And she would just say, "A terrible, beastly man." . . . About six months afterwards she said that she didn't believe that it had been an accident. She thought that it had been planned. Well, you can't plan something like that. And that, you know, sent me down the steps of that Watergate just laughing and kicking and screaming.

Maureen Bunyan genuinely dislikes the professional interview situation when there is "any kind of phoniness or set-up": "I can't say I'm crazy about interviewing professional celebrities. I had to interview Raquel Welch once when I had to ask her to button up her blouse and I felt so stupid!"

Pauline Frederick had difficulty singling out her greatest satisfaction over the years:

> There have been so many, because I have been here through all the crises. I've been at the United Nations since the beginning, so each one to me was the greatest opportunity, starting with the Korean War when I was on the air day and night during the six weeks when it was a crisis at the United Nations. . . . The Middle East War, the Cuban missile crisis, Suez, Hungary, the Chinese coming into the UN— they've all been very exciting, and at the time they seemed to me to be the most satisfying. But then another crisis would come up. . . .

The recognition that stems from working in the television medium was a source of satisfaction to many women in our group. Lynn Sherr explains: "The added thing about television is that there's the ham in me. I love it. I like being on camera and I like being recognized in the street."

Gloria Rojas and I went to the same junior high school. She remembered, but to my shame I did not. During our interview Gloria told me why television broadcasting brings her such fulfillment:

> I love it. It's an ego trip. I really wanted to be somebody, desperately, all my life. . . . Remember we were talking about why I remember you? I probably remember you because you were what I wanted to be. I never had a part in a play. Nobody knew who

> I was. I went back to my high school reunion. They all knew me from *now,* but they didn't remember that I was in their class. I was like a complete washout. I wanted [recognition] desperately, and I find I'm enjoying it *tremendously.*

Melba Tolliver is not particularly pleased with the on-camera aspect of her work. She says, "I suppose the least rewarding is what would seem the most rewarding, and that's going on the air. . . . You're just sitting in the studio talking to a camera and you can't see the people." This reaction is all the more interesting considering the fact that Melba Tolliver is a full-fledged star, someone the public identifies with and cares about. One male television agent describes her as "probably the biggest star in New York, man or woman." An ABC producer commented: "Even bigots accept her. With Melba, color doesn't exist. The people mob her." Yet Melba Tolliver believes that the power to cause change remains behind the scenes in the television world and not on camera. What she regards as most satisfying in her job are "personal interviews with people, without a camera, which doesn't happen very often. Relating to people on a one-to-one basis is what I find the most rewarding."

dissatisfactions of job. The most frequently mentioned dissatisfaction of the television reporter involved the pressure of time demands in the profession, both as it related to personal lives and as it affected the ability to present the best possible story. Rebecca Bell echoes the feelings of many television newswomen who find it necessary to give all of their lives to their jobs:

> There is no personal life. I am on call twenty-four hours, seven days a week. I go five weeks or more

> without a day off, most of the time out of town. I am on three or four planes a week. It is impossible to make any plans whatsoever, even as much as a casual dinner date. . . . If you're needed and they ask you to cover a story, you don't say, "I won't go."

The pressure to get stories on the air quickly results in tension and in much frustration to many women in broadcasting. Lynn Sherr describes the problem of the short, one-day stories for which the reporter must become an instant expert during a half-hour car ride to the story site: "Like a bunch of headlines, you can't say much, just report a situation. You can't sink your teeth into it. You can't make much of an impact."

Gloria Rojas specifies the particularly acute dissatisfaction that stems from being "used":

> Somebody wants a little free publicity. . . . A man adopts a block in East Harlem and sends out press releases. He brings paint, a steel band, etc. When the cameras stopped rolling, the band stopped playing, and people stopped painting. I felt used. I felt dirty. . . . We went back a few weeks later and the place was dirty. It was the same. . . . This man got a lot of free publicity. I find this so low and so inexcusable. But it's so easy to get suckered into that.

Barbara Walters admits that she finds herself dissatisfied:

> At least once a week with assignments over the air, I find here I am again doing just the [same] sort of silly female assignment—the whole feeling of a woman being second place on this program. I think if you sit around and become bitter about it you lose your sense of humor and your ability on the air. And I know that I'm hired on the "Today" program be-

cause I'm a woman, and they want to have a kind of softness and femininity, and hope that you look nice. But I find that sometimes when we're doing a news interview out of Washington, I never ask the question until after [the late] Frank McGee does. . . . Most of the serious interviews I don't do unless I go out and get them myself, which is one of the reasons that I try to do filmed stories, because if I do, then it's my interview. And if it comes into the studio then it's an interview that I may or may not share. This is not the fault of the host of the program. It's the way everyone automatically regards the role of the woman on the show.

skills and qualities necessary for success.

Pinpointing career success remains difficult in the volatile world of television news. The question of what skills or qualities were necessary for achieving success in the broadcasting profession yielded an interesting juxtaposition of responses from our news reporters. The women were evenly divided in their belief that achievement in their field demands competence, perseverance, hard work, and plain luck. Gloria Rojas believes in the importance of "timing and persistence" and in the "blind chance":

> Being at the right place at the right time is probably the most important. Let me give you an example: my friend Geraldo [Rivera] [11] and Willowbrook. . . . Channel 5 had it in the can but unedited when Channel 7 put it on the air that night. It became Geraldo's story, right? Everybody associates Geraldo with it

[11] Gloria Rojas was the person who suggested that Geraldo Rivera go into the news business. She told him of the opening at WABC-TV for a Puerto Rican reporter. In the fall of 1974, she joined WABC-TV herself.

. . . so that made him. That was the right place at the right time. But, of course, if he didn't have anything behind it, it wouldn't have lasted. Sheer luck will pull you to the forefront. If I discovered a major scandal today—let me see, what would a major scandal be? If I discovered that Henry Kissinger was really a spy, don't you think everyone would know it across the country by tomorrow? But it might be just luck that I had discovered it.

Marlene Sanders considers competence essential but describes luck as the outstanding asset:

I really think luck is very important because you can have two equally talented people and if one of them goes into an environment which is really hostile, nothing she can do is going to help. In the early years, I worked for very good people, men who really didn't care that I was female. . . . There was opportunity to be upwardly mobile, which a lot of people don't have. So I was lucky in the first people I worked for and I got through the first five years making great career advances. And that was partly because I was doing a good job. I worked very hard, very long hours. I liked what I was doing. I was enthusiastic and I hope intelligent about it. But I also had people around who were not a hindrance, because you do run into them at certain points in your career, and sometimes that's a very difficult problem.

Pat Collins advocates the need for good health and stamina to withstand the heavy work load:

Stamina is very important. You simply cannot work these long hours day after day, month after month, without a break unless you're in really good health, unless your stamina is good and unless you want to do it very badly. . . . I'm suspicious of people in this business who manage to lead glamorous lives. . . . If they really are up until 3:00 in the morning, either they're drinking the blood of seven snakes and they've discovered some new potion no one knows about. Or they really aren't doing their homework, they're faking it and they've got people to help them fake it, and I suspect it's the last one.

Several newswomen emphasized the importance of a deep commitment to reporting. One network correspondent described it as "the feeling in your gut" that makes you want to do it, that makes the reporter willing to make the necessary sacrifices, to accept the disappointments and defeats that are part of the broadcasting profession.

Sally Quinn's personal experience in television [12] caused her to stress self-confidence as a criterion for success:

You've got to have self-confidence. If I didn't have an enormous amount of self-confidence, I would have been destroyed by this whole experience. . . . The pressures have been enormous on me, especially with the publicity buildup. . . . You can't learn to be a perfect anchorwoman in one day, and I knew that I was not going to be perfect and that people were just going to crucify me because I wasn't perfect. . . . But there was nothing I could do about it; I only knew I had to keep thinking that I was good and that I would get better.

12 After unfavorable ratings and reviews greeted her co-anchor position on "The CBS Morning News," Sally Quinn left CBS to return to the *Washington Post* in March 1974.

The men in management uniformly responded that proven reportorial skills were the prime prerequisite for success in their profession. They placed the major emphasis on writing ability. Av Westin succinctly states: "The first thing I look for is an ability to write." But television reporting requires clear, lucid script writing and not beautiful magazine prose. The difference is described by Trish Reilly, who found the transition from *Newsweek* to television difficult:

> The way I write is not the way you write for television. . . . After one of my early pieces, our executive producer sat me down and said, "Look Trish, you are a very good writer. Now I know it's going to be hard, but you just have to get over it!"

Melba Tolliver explains that good news writing is "not just sitting down at the typewriter":

> You don't need to be Ernest Hemingway or Ralph Ellison, because it's not that kind of writing. . . . It's thinking of ways to present events in a clear, concise, understandable way. Hopefully it's also entertaining and everything else it needs to be to grab an audience. . . . That's one of the most difficult things for me. It always has been and I guess it will be forever.

This emphasis on writing competence concurs with an earlier survey in which writing ability was the most often mentioned skill sought by news directors when hiring reporters.[13] The next most frequently mentioned set of skills dealt with some aspect of on-air presentation. In my own interviews, the ability to communicate effectively was consistently stressed by leading news executives.

13 Irving E. Fang and Frank W. Gerval, "Survey of Hiring Preferences in Television News," *Journal of Broadcasting,* 15 (Fall 1971), 431.

Sally Quinn, former co-host, "CBS Morning News."

Al Primo, ABC News, outlines his standards for broadcasting success:

> The first thing that you look for is a sufficient background, reportorial ability. We're blessed in New York with being in the market that it seems everyone wants to work for, so many of the applicants come to us with a proven track record. . . . For WABC-TV, New York, what I tried to do was to bring a higher level of reporter into the station, because we felt that

in order for the audience to give us their attention after years of benign neglect in the news area, we ought to have the very best news reporters. So rather than hire correspondents in other cities, I decided that everyone who worked on our staff will have had at least ten years of experience, not only as a reporter, but as an anchorman. That is, [will be] an on-air performer in addition to being a reporter. . . . I think that in 1973, television has become so sophisticated that not only must you be able to have the intellectual capabilities to be a reporter, but you have to have creative talents in communication to succeed and be effective on television. So we're looking for a very rare breed. The man or woman must not only be a good reporter but be able to communicate very well.

Very often, theory and actual practice produce differing results, as Ted Kavenau readily admits:

Theoretically you look for a reporter who has had experience, because New York is a number one market. . . . You hope they have somewhat of a performing talent, since this is a performing business as well as journalism. You have to have some kind of charisma. . . . That's the formula. Now in truth, often people get hired for a variety of reasons. . . . You fire somebody; at that moment somebody else is sitting around and you grab them. So those are the informal things and often the informal will take precedence over the formal. If somebody walks in when you have a real need, they're much more likely to get hired even if much better people happen to be around when there's no need for someone.

The words of one male news executive sum up every news director's dream:

> I need a seasoned reporter. Someone that's been in the news business, who's capable of operating as a professional immediately. . . . After that, I look for someone with a personality, a sense of humor. Good looking on the air, of course. We're selling a product. And, hopefully, someone who can write extremely well and is willing to work fourteen hours a day for little money. A paragon is what I search for. . . .

With few exceptions, the women in television news are very bright and exceedingly attractive, with energetic personalities and strong professional self-images. They work with uniform diligence and determination in the pursuit of excellence. Indeed, they may best be described as "paragons."

4
being a woman in television news

advantages and disadvantages. As in other male-dominated professions, women in television news have great visibility simply because they remain a small and conspicuous minority in their field. This visibility is often a double-edged sword, at one time offering help, at another time presenting a hindrance. As we explore the issues relating to sexual differences and professional standards, we see how the ability to work effectively in the broadcasting profession is directly affected by membership in the female sex.

Being a woman is a trait that is manifest, and many of the women I spoke with claimed that their sex was a definite advantage to them in achieving their professional goals. Fifty percent of our newswomen admitted that being a woman had been a positive factor in their being hired for their jobs.

Each of these women felt that her respective television station was obviously looking to increase the number of on-air women in their ranks at the time she was hired. Most were grateful for the advantage that their sex provided. Several of the women frankly concede a willingness to use feminine qualities to further achieve their professional aims. Sylvia Chase surprisingly admits:

> I never would have gotten this job without being a woman. . . . I feel my qualifications at the time of entry into the job were not such that I would have received it had I not been a dame. I had no experience in television whatsoever. But you'll find that in television news. I mean, guys will get hired for oddball reasons, too. But I definitely think the fact that I was a woman enabled me to get the job. . . . Many times people will feel that I'm not going to be hard on them, or that kind of thing. And a lot of times I'm very sweet and friendly and naïve-seeming, and I just carry people along. And all of the sudden, wham! I got you there! My feeling is—God damn it, I've had to pay so much for being a woman, it's been such a tremendous disadvantage to me, that I'll use it any time I can.

Ann Medina openly declares that being a woman is a help:

> Obviously I would like to think that I'm hired for competence, rather than just being a token. But I'm realistic enough to know the fact I'm a woman is a very nice thing. Just like the fact I have a Spanish surname is a very nice thing to have on your employment records . . . even though I'm as WASP as they come. . . . All these are factors, but being a woman definitely is a bigger factor.

Sylvia Chase with Hughes Rudd, CBS News.

The only other area frequently cited as presenting an advantage to the working newswomen is in dealing with certain people who do not view women as a threat. Consequently, these people tend to be more open and trusting than they would be with a male reporter. Pat Collins explains:

> There are invariably those men who will say things to you that they wouldn't say to a man. And by that, I don't mean that they do it because they think they can date you. . . . It's like when you meet a stranger on an airplane, you end up telling them everything. Why? Because a stranger is not very threatening. . . . Up until now your advantage is that they will blurt out things they would never think of blurt-

> ing out to a man because they don't think you'll un-
> derstand the importance or the magnitude. . . .
> Then, if you trip them up, then they start to get wor-
> ried.

Several women reporters mentioned the fact that it is easier for an attractive female to catch the eye of a politician. Many politicians, particularly Southerners, will grant an interview to a woman where they would turn down a man. This is a decided advantage to a television news reporter. Lesley Stahl comments:

> There are still some men around Washington, in office, who just can't be rude to a woman. They just can't do it. They were raised to be polite to women, especially Southern gentlemen. . . . They are more likely to stop and talk to a woman, the first time. . . . It's your one-shot deal with a guy. I know the first time that Henry Kissinger ever saw me, he gave me an interview where he hadn't given one to anybody else; a straight "no-comment" situation. He gave me an interview, and then the second time he saw me, he didn't.

While one-third of the women interviewed felt there were no advantages at all to being a woman in the broadcasting profession, only half that number said there were no disadvantages to being a member of the female sex. The large majority of the group felt their sex was a definite handicap to them in their work. Primarily because the broadcasting profession is peopled mostly by men, many newswomen felt the constant need to fight preconceived notions of what a woman can do and what she looks right doing. One newswoman preferred to express her deeply felt views anonymously:

I don't think men respect women. . . . I don't think they really respect their opinions. I don't think they really respect their ability to do a job. And, therefore, when it comes to the business of hiring somebody, they're always sort of hanging back and suspicious whether the woman would actually be able to do it. Meantime, these people that are doing this to you are people that you swamped when you were going through school. I don't mean that in a bitter way. I mean this is a fact of life.

Marlene Sanders feels that being a woman in the profession has made advancement basically "a struggle":

If you're competent and nobody will give you a break, you're just a dead duck. . . . People are only competent if they have the opportunity to become so. That means job advancement. With women's groups active at all the networks now, there are actual steps being worked out so that people can advance, so they can be trained, so they can move from one category to another, and not depend on the whim of some guy. I mean, maybe he is terrific. I did work for some terrific guys early on. But maybe he's a bum. . . .

There is a whole unattractive and deprecating vocabulary that goes with women who work. No single word reflects this double standard more than "aggressive." While the necessity of being aggressive is traditionally considered a prerequisite for success in television news, many newswomen were quick to note the unpleasant connotation of the word.

Lynn Sherr admits to being aggressive by nature:

> It's the way I am. I mean aggressive in a good way. I don't know how you mean it. I'm ambitious. I'm aggressive. In the past if a woman did something she would be called an aggressive broad, and if a man did it he would be an ambitious career man.

Working journalists are required to get the story—one way or another. One of the most aggressive newswomen on record was Anne Royall, who managed to get an interview with President John Quincy Adams by simply sitting on his clothes while the President was bathing in the Potomac. She just refused to leave until he spoke with her.[1] Not many reporters would shrink from such an effective interview technique today.

Barbara Walters offers interesting insights into her own evaluation of aggressiveness in television:

> You can be terribly aggressive on the air and not be off the air. . . . I used to watch the news conferences with all the reporters when they're interviewing the President and I would think, "I'd never raise my hand. Suppose I'd raise my hand and I'd say something stupid. I'd sooner die." It's very hard for me to make a phone call and set up an interview. I write letters and I talk to myself—and yet, I would be considered aggressive, I guess. . . . I think when I actually ask questions, my *questions* might be considered aggressive in that they are penetrating, I would hope, or to the point. It still is, no matter what they say, a dirty word for a woman and an attractive word for a man. A man should be aggressive and a woman shouldn't.

1 Winzola McLendon and Scottie Smith, *Don't Quote Me* (New York: Dutton, 1970), p. 168.

Gloria Rojas is sometimes bothered by audience reaction to her aggressiveness:

> If I'm as aggressive as I think I should be in a particular situation, a lot of people get annoyed or write in and ask me, "Don't I know how ladies behave?". . . I think I'm damn nice. I like myself and I think that should be good enough for everyone else.

Pat Collins is not happy about her need to be "very aggressive" on story assignments: "You must be willing to walk over people. It's not very nice and I don't like it very much." As is often the case in the broadcasting world, what is merely necessary for a man becomes a necessary evil for a woman.

Newswomen strongly feel an obligation to prove themselves. As a result of not being looked upon as the equal of men, many women feel the need to demonstrate their worth and even to be "better than a man" in their work. Virginia Sherwood attests to this

> having to prove that you can do it, not because you're a woman, but because you're a reporter and because that's what you want to do. I think the big disadvantage is the prejudice that is not there because they "don't want a woman," but is something that has been created over the years. It's custom. Women are new in this field. Really they shouldn't be, but they are—as women are new in a lot of fields. It's beginning to open up a great deal, but first of all, I think, you almost have to prove that you're better—not as good, but better.

Marya McLaughlin believes that the basic disadvantage to being a woman is her conspicuousness:

> Just simply because we're sort of elephants with hats on or something. We're just sort of a strange breed in the business in television news. In that respect everything you do stands out. . . . You are under intense criticism and pressure.

Barbara Walters sits at the pinnacle of the television news world and still experiences difficulties stemming from her sex:

> You have to work harder. It's been said before, but it's true. You are taken less seriously and you are very often scorned by your own co-workers, who say, "Well, obviously she got that story because he liked her personally." I think that my own interview with Dr. Kissinger— I don't think that the fact I was a female, in spite of his reputation, had anything to do with my getting the story. You have to fight harder for the serious stories. I still do. . . . It's a tougher job for a woman because a woman has to be awfully good. She really does. A man can be much more excused. I never felt as miserable or as vulnerable or as frightened as I did in China when I was the only on-the-air woman. And I'm sure everybody thinks—the people I worked with, probably—that I was all very cool and calm and controlled. It was the most desperate situation that I can recall. I never worked as hard or felt as conscious of the mistakes I could make. . . . I came home expecting to be fired. It was that kind of anxiety.

A few of the women often complained of being the first to be assigned "soft" news or feature stories. While this may often be as much a consideration of experience as it is a result of sexual stereotyping, there are frequently times when women are assigned stories on the basis of traditional sex-defined roles. Theresa Brown discussed her problems during the meat boycott in New York:

> I'm the only woman reporter they have, so I get all the meat boycott stories and all the meatless food stories. . . . Actually, I've only cooked three meals in my life. The most uncomfortable place for me in the whole world is in a kitchen. And when I feel most insecure is when I'm doing these food stories. . . . I have no idea what's going on. I think that's a disadvantage because I hate to do food stories. If I were a man, they wouldn't assign them to me.

Among newswomen, lack of familiarity with home-centered specialties is more often the rule than the exception. Pat Collins remarked with good-humored frankness: "There's nobody in this shop [WNBC-TV] who's really a woman's woman reporter, that is, someone who really knows everything there is to know about fashion and cooking. . . . You'd be lucky to get a square meal out of any of us [*laugh*]. I'm the worst at it. They can at least fake. I'm not even good at that." This practice of assigning stories to women reporters on the basis of their sexual roles is best explained by a male news executive at CBS who prefers to remain anonymous:

> What has happened in some cases is that against their wills, women have been typecast into doing certain types of stories. As a producer goes over a broadcast, he is constantly weighing something that does exist and that is the counterbalance of the serious with the light or the human-interest part of the broadcast. This is an entertainment medium that we are operating in, and someone can't do sixty minutes of gore and violence with sports and weather thrown in. There are certain areas in the broadcast

where we say we will do a light [feature], an up-beat feature. I think many, many times, probably more often than we should, we have the women reporters do that light. And I think a lot of people, I think Pia Lindstrom, if you get to interview her,[2] would object to this. If you look at the things that women reporters do in this market, I think most of them are doing a fairly healthy balance of light stories and very serious stories. And God knows, I think there are some stories that women do better. . . .

Sixty percent of the men interviewed for this study said there was no advantage at all to being a woman in broadcasting. Of the remaining 40 percent of the male sample, Ted Kavenau was the most unreserved in his views concerning the advantages of women in the television profession:

The advantages are that you can get a job because you're female, because everyone needs a token female. . . . Most of them are miserable. They couldn't report their way out of a paper bag. The benefit of women sometimes is if they're good-looking or amiable, men will speak to them. . . . A man will sit and talk to them and they can charm him. In other words, Mata Hari. It's the Mata Hari thing. If the devil can't succeed, send a woman. A woman knows how to use her looks and her charm or what she can, to get things. They'll talk. But if you put a woman on a hard story, in most cases, where they've really got to sweat and hustle, drive and use imagination, they're almost useless. . . . I think the more opportunities there are for women in broadcasting, the worse it is. It'll destroy the business.

2 In our interview, Pia Lindstrom seemed to feel this was true mainly at the outset of her career.

Twenty percent of the male executives expressed the belief that being a woman presented no particular disadvantages within the television news world. Eighty percent of the men readily admitted to the various problems women face in their male-dominated profession. An NBC Vice-President described the disadvantages as being basically the fact that "the world is still being run by men. There is no confidence in being in the hands of a female. There remains the vestige of built-in resistance to femaleness." Al Ittleson feels the problem is within the woman herself:

> I think some of the disadvantages are built into the psyche of women. I think women have considered themselves to be secondary people. They have an awful lot to overcome within themselves, let alone to overcome with a six-foot-five sound man and a fat lighting man and a reactionary cameraman. That fight they can do, once they settle the problem they have within themselves.

Av Westin deliberates on the personality problems presented by certain women reporters in the field:

> Some women whom I've encountered or some whom I've observed . . . they haven't worked out their own image. Are they one of the boys? They're cursing like hell and they're trying to belt it back à la *Front Page*. Or are they one of the girls and trying to be gay, feminine, and sprightly? And they're not sure themselves. And in a funny way it means that I have to sort of adjust on Monday, "Are you Miss Goody Two-Shoes?" And on Tuesday, "Are you Sam the truck driver?" . . . I'm thinking of one woman correspondent at NBC who plays that game and just drives the guys she works with out of their minds

because they don't know which way they're going. And that's a problem. And in this business, the fewer the problems you have, [the better,] given the fact that you've got to cover the news every day and react quickly and spend a lot of money and guess right or guess wrong. The last thing you need is hassles that are built in because of somebody's personality.

The men in management were equally divided on the question involving inappropriate assignments for women reporters. Half of the male executives interviewed said there were no assignments in the field that were inappropriate for women to cover. Of those who disagreed, most felt a greater responsibility for a woman's safety on dangerous assignments. One news director gives sincere expression to these sentiments:

Out in the field of cold work, in the middle of a confrontation at the school site (which are television staples), a picket line, a union meeting, a woman is at a disadvantage in one respect. . . . The desk is worried she's going to get her head handed to her. She is at a small advantage when things aren't too bad out there. People are not going to beat on her quite as rapidly. The cops normally won't belt a woman reporter unless things get bad. . . . There are a lot of stories in television that are in a male atmosphere, locker rooms in sports for one. More than that, going down in the subway tunnel, going into the water tunnel they're building up here. These are hazardous situations which you don't want to throw a woman into. And there's no advantage to their being there. . . . You take responsibility for your people when you get them out in the street. And if there's shooting coming, I'm not liberated enough to figure, well, if she gets shot, she gets shot. If he gets shot, O.K. If she gets shot, that's not nice!

Sam Zelman, CBS News, allows the decision to rest with the reporter:

> Sometimes news stories take our people into areas where public safety is threatened. Some news people are required to work odd hours and in cities where street violence is common. We may have a touch more concern for the woman out on her own than the man. . . . But if the woman tells us that's not a factor, then it becomes her problem.

Ted Kavenau is an outspoken advocate of separatism based on sex-role distinctions:

> I believe that there are sex roles and if you put a woman into a role which is suitable for her sex, she'll deliver. . . . If you put them on certain stories where they're chasing murders and crime and so forth and so on, they become masculinized. They lower their voices and try to imitate David Brinkley. You get these female-men on the air trying to look cool, look hard, and look knowing and do the thing that men have done. . . . If they do things for which they are uniquely qualified . . . they perform well.

In direct opposition is Al Primo, who emphasizes competence as the key to effective reporting:

> I don't think that anything is inappropriate for a woman to cover. As a matter of fact, a good reporter can cover any story. That's one of the tributes and measuring devices that we apply to all reporters. We send our reporters out on a variety of stories all the time. The very good reporters always come back with the story. And the average reporters sometimes don't come back with a story and say there's not a story

> there. But I know in my heart that if there is a good reporter sent to a story, he will come back with it.

None of the women believed her sex was a negative factor on story assignments. Many said they had covered riot and semiriot situations and felt confident that they could handle a dangerous story as effectively as a man. Rebecca Bell declares with the assurance born of experience:

> In the cities where I worked where the crews know me, they know I've got sense enough to take care of myself. They take care of their job and I take care of mine. Once, that time in New York when I was on loan, I was new. I was there three days and went out and covered a semiriot. This was a brand new crew. They didn't know me. They didn't know I had covered a riot before and that I knew how to protect myself. They were worried. . . . I've got enough common sense to know that if the riot breaks through the police lines, you move. A man or a woman, you don't stand there, you move.

Ann Medina describes her experience while covering the 1972 presidential conventions:

> The night of Nixon's winning the nomination, they assigned me to probably the worst corner as far as the action goes. . . . They were concerned. I was without a gas mask. I was even getting sprayed by the gas, I was so close, probably for two hours. They were concerned, but they treated me like a person, you know, not like a frail, fragile woman.

Connie Chung has covered riots and states succinctly: "A man's head will crack as easily as a woman's! Tear gas affects a man or a woman just the same!"

During a shoot-out in a Black Muslim mosque in Harlem on April 14, 1972, that year's first major racial disturbance, Pat Collins received a "kick in the head" that sent her to the hospital. In their front page coverage of the melee, the *New York Times* reported: "Local youths roughed up Pat Collins, a white woman on the staff of NBC News, and threw her to the ground." [3] The experience failed to dampen Pat's enthusiasm for her work or her willingness to cover similar riot situations.

Phyllis Haynes spoke to me of physical strength and the sexes: "I have a black belt in karate and I think the whole attitude on the inferiority of female strength is an invention of males. We are not only strong, but have the element of surprise on our side."

Theresa Brown offers another perspective to the problem of personal danger on assignments:

> If we're in Harlem, let's say, and there's a building, there'll be buildings that all of them are afraid to go in. . . . Now, because I'm black, I don't care about the building. To me it's just a building with black people inside. And so I'll go in in a minute and try to find out what the story is, whereas they'll hold back. They won't go into the building. . . . At that point my blackness takes over and they forget about my being a woman. . . . If we're in another situation where there may be some trouble but it's not in a black area, then they'll say, "Oh, Theresa, we think we'd better go in with you."

Lesley Stahl comments: "I think that when it gets down to a choice between getting some really good film and protecting me, they'd go for the film!"

The single exception raised by several women correspondents that can present a real threat to the newswoman

3 *New York Times,* April 15, 1972, p. 16.

and not to the newsman is the problem of rape. Sally Quinn explains:

> Obviously, sending a woman out alone at night is going to be a problem because women can be raped and men can't. I mean even at the *Washington Post* we had escorts sometimes taking us back and forth to the garage where we parked. . . . In the case of television, you usually have a crew, so it wouldn't matter that much anyway.

The credibility of women journalists doing sports stories has always created heated debate. Women in the locker room remains a big emotional issue. When two female newspaper reporters were invited by the coaches of both National Hockey League All-Star teams to enter the dressing rooms for the first time, big headlines and frenzied opposition were the reaction. The New York Rangers' wives were so upset, they asked that their husbands petition to keep women out of the locker room. The Rangers voted to limit women to areas outside the room. The Boston Bruins are the only team with an official open-door policy.[4]

Linda Shen relates that the most fun she ever had was on a sports story: "They gave it to me only out of desperation. I was supposed to do an interview in a locker room in Madison Square Garden, but of course, when I got there they wouldn't let me into the locker room. I loved doing it—the shock value."

Marlene Sanders did the sports as part of her three-month anchor assignment on the Saturday night edition of the ABC "Weekend News":

> I happen to know a considerable amount about sports. I didn't make any goofs. It might have jarred

4 Robin Herman, "Reporter's Notebook: A Look at Equal Rights and Hockey," *New York Times,* February 9, 1975, sec. 5, p. 1.

some viewers, and it will jar them the first time or the first few times. But they'll get used to it. If they never have the opportunity to get used to it, they will always be jarred. And that's been the reason that women have been kept off the air—that their voices aren't authoritative, that they have no credibility, that they won't be taken seriously, that they're not authority figures.

Melba Tolliver has covered sports stories with complete effectiveness:

> Women have been brought up along certain lines. There's no way you can erase that. A lot of women have not been brought up to be interested in sports. But, I've done sports stories and I haven't had people write any letters of protest because they don't believe me, because in many instances, I got my information from the same place [the men] did, from the wire services.

Melba's bosses take pride in her ability to handle sports stories with believability. Al Primo stated with obvious satisfaction:

> We were the station that sent Melba Tolliver down to spring training to get what I consider to be probably the best spring training report that we've ever had, in the sense that she was able to look at it in a different way and to relate in a broader sense. . . . She got a story that didn't require a tremendous background by the audience to understand. We use male reporters on fashion stories as well as women, and in all cases, I think, the same qualifications apply—if they have a good story, they'll come back with it.

Av Westin is concerned that women doing sports, or a man doing fashions, makes the story "a curiosity":

> It detracts just a bit by its oddity from what we really should be in the business of doing, which is conveying information. . . . The audience itself, and that's our client, a certain minuscule percentage of their consciousness would be distracted from the content by the anomaly of the reverse roles in those particular fields.

Kenneth MacQueen thinks this credibility factor can be overcome by "superior delivery and participation." He speaks of a case in point:

> We've looked at a woman in the South who is very unique as a sportscaster. But the reasons that she's unique are the same reasons that would apply to anybody. She is gifted with looks. She is an excellent communicator. She has a great interest in sports. She gets involved deeply with it, so that her content is superior, and consequently does an outstanding job.

When competence truly becomes the cornerstone for accomplishment, the men and women in broadcasting will be closer to setting professional standards that will become the model for all people in all professions.

crews: working together.

The three-man camera crew, consisting of a cameraman, a light man, and a sound man, is an indispensable part of the television news operation. Betty Rollin wrote her personal description of technical crews for the *New York Times:*

Without them you can do nothing. Nothing. As I said earlier, all of one's little perceptions and profound understandings of the story at hand are magnificently useless unless the camera's rolling, the sound is recording, and the lights are on. The point is *you* don't get the story. The *crew* gets the story, or no story. . . . I guess what I like best about crews is that they are a) good company and b) straight shooters. Unlike many of the folks from my old life, crews do not, as they say, put on airs. They are what they are—Archie Bunker on the outside, pussycat on the inside—and that's nice.[5]

While many of the crews were openly pleased at being called "pussycat," I found that newswomen and crews often reacted to one another along more traditional behavioral lines. The male-female interactions that present the most difficulty to women reporters are these relationships with members of the technical crew. Many newswomen rely on feminine qualities assumed to be part of the sex role in order to deal most effectively with the men. Theresa Brown explains the problem:

You're not working with your pseudo-liberated male. You're working with your very down-to-earth basic man. And these men all believe a woman's place is in the home, barefoot and pregnant. They really do. They all told me that. . . . They're great guys, but that's where they believe she belongs.

Sylvia Chase is pleased with her ability as a woman to work well with the crew. She feels her relationships are "much better" than those enjoyed by male correspondents:

5 Betty Rollin, "So Now I Know From Pastrami," *New York Times,* January 21, 1973, p. 17.

> You know a lot of women feel, I'm not going to play the woman's role, but I do. I think the best thing about women is that they're soft, gentle, kindly, considerate creatures. . . . Well hell, I was brought up like an old fashioned girl and that's where I am. When I'm out with my crew, I take good care of them. If I'm working them very hard, I try to bring them coffee or a coke. I hug them and I laugh and I joke with them and I really try to make them feel good. And that's something I can do uniquely as a woman. A man can't kiss his cameraman, but I do.

Rose Ann Scamardella believes the crew is protective of her because she is a woman:

> The crews are very, very easy and very pleasant to work with. I think that's an advantage of being a woman. They feel sorry for me when we're out in the cold. When we're out in a dangerous situation, they're very protective. . . . They've been extremely helpful to me because I'm a woman. They give me tips. They take direction from me fine. I have no problem with them as far as doing what I tell them to do. If they disagree, they'll tell me why. More than anything, they're trying to help. They have the attitude that I'm a woman and should be protected rather than I'm a woman and I'm stupid.

The WABC-TV crews I worked with do respond to Rose Ann's ready smile and sunny disposition. One cameraman told me while on assignment with Rose Ann: "She's O.K., so we'll go out of our way for her."

Trish Reilly frankly admits to using "feminine wiles" in working with members of the crew:

Rose Ann Scamardella,
WABC-TV "Eyewitness News."

I definitely think a woman can use her femininity
and her sweetness to get these guys to work with
her. And it's crucial. You have to do it. This is one of
the things that all the correspondents made really
clear to me, that you have to get these crews to work
with you, because if they resent you, if they don't like
you, they can sabotage you in a million ways. . . .
The way you play upon chauvinism is by being sweet
and feminine.

Marlene Sanders has experienced little difficulty in her
many years of working with film crews. She prides herself on
the ability to treat men and women "just the same":

Most of the time [I've] worked one hundred percent with men and we have always been good buddies. I say that in the sense that occasionally a guy will make a pass at you. But all right, that happens and you have to deal with that in life anyhow. Basically we've gotten along very well. I don't use femininity. I don't think I ever have to try to advance. . . . I just have tried to be myself and to do the job. . . . I probably have more in common with the men I worked with than I would have with their wives. . . . It's a cooperative venture, anyhow, and if you don't get along with your crew, you're not going to get any good results.

The crews themselves were critical of many women reporters for an inability to withstand pressure. "Women are more changeable, more tempermental," commented one cameraman. Another crew member confided to me: "In our shop a woman has always been the cause of a crew guy loosing his job. They're quick to run back to mama complaining."

When adequate ability can be demonstrated, resistance to the acceptance of the woman reporter is measurably reduced. Pauline Frederick describes her working relationships during her distinguished career:

I have been treated as a reporter. Of course, at the very beginning, and that was years ago, I was somewhat of a curiosity because I was the only woman broadcasting news. . . . But as I tried to be professional in what I was doing, I found I was being treated as a professional, which I think is terribly important.

If a woman is a real professional in the eyes of the camera crew, she is accepted completely. In personal discussions with members of working crews, the main criterion demanded of the male and female reporters was competence in the field, the ability to make quick decisions whenever necessary. One cameraman told me: "There's no difference between a man and a woman in the field. The really important thing is the ability of the reporter to make on-the-spot decisions. If they know their business, it doesn't matter what sex they are."

Camera crews work as a team. They are protective of one another and are straight and direct in their dealings with others. Most are competent professionals, eager to help, and most often their help is invaluable. Since all have differing personalities, it is necessary for the news reporter, who is officially the "boss" of the crew, to deal sensitively and intelligently with the inevitable problems arising on the job. Learning to deal effectively with people becomes a basic necessity in the television news world.

Often a man will tend to overreact as much as the women with whom they come into professional contact. An interesting example of supersensitivity to the potential problems of male-female interaction occurred when Pia Lindstrom became the first woman in the news department at KGO-TV in San Francisco, over the intense objections of the news director, who was then Roger Grimsby. Today, Roger Grimsby is the anchorman of WABC-TV's "Eyewitness News." He admits to having made a mistake:

> I trembled at the thought of having a very attractive lady in the newsroom. As it turned out, I couldn't have been more wrong. Pia was perfect; cool and reserved and competent. She came in there with a minimum of experience. She had been doing a talk show in the morning on the same station before she came into the newsroom. But she had no experience with film. But she learned her basic film skills within three weeks and from that time on just took off and

was a perfect lady. Now, the wrong girl in that milieu—it could have been disaster. But she was perfect.

Another influential male executive today admits his error concerning the acceptance of women in the broadcasting profession. Reuven Frank, while President of NBC News,[6] was widely quoted in 1971 as saying: "I have the strong feeling that audiences are less prepared to accept news from a woman's voice than from a man's." [7] When I interviewed Mr. Frank, I discovered that he had modified his views:

For a long time I thought and was quoted and it was thrown in my teeth that I did not think the American public was ready to accept a woman. We live on acceptance. If they don't accept us, they turn us off. There is no theoretical or ethical goal that we can aspire to that can counteract that. People don't watch what they have to. They watch what they like. . . . I think they have now been conditioned—and all it is is a process of conditioning and development—so that in reporting they will take it. I don't know who's going to take the first chance on a woman in a major anchor position. It'll be interesting to find out. . . . Of course, that kind of job falls open so rarely. It's only a tenth of one percent of the people in the field who do that kind of work, even on the local level. . . . I was toying with the idea for a while. The trap here is you put somebody on because she's a woman. When you're facing a man, you say you've got eleven men and one of them is good and one of them is fair and the other nine couldn't hack

6 Reuven Frank is now Senior Executive Producer for NBC News.

7 Quoted in *Newsweek,* August 30, 1971, p. 63.

it. And so the factor that it's a man is not part of your consideration, at least not a conscious part.

I asked Mr. Frank if the phenomenal success of the news team of Chet Huntley and David Brinkley would have been possible with a female as co-anchor. Without hesitation, he responded: "It couldn't have happened between anyone other than David and Chet."

I later asked Roger Grimsby if he felt his success on "Eyewitness News" would be as great with a woman as his co-anchor. He replied:

> I'd much rather sit next to a girl than I would Bill Beutel. But I'm sure he feels the same way. But that's interesting. I don't know. I don't know whether the audience would accept that and don't ask me why. It's tradition. It's what they're used to. . . . I would hesitate to make a joke to a girl or get cute with a girl much more so than I would with Bill Beutel, for that reason. And, again, it's not what I think. It's what I think the public thinks. Then, what I thought about Pia Lindstrom was wrong, so maybe I'm wrong about this thing.[8]

The problem appears to rest on who will be the one to take the lead. If management led, indications are that the audience would be willing to accept women in anchor positions. It is doubtful, however, that audiences will begin demanding more women on the air. That kind of pressure is being exerted today by recent regulations of the government and the FCC and by

8 WABC-TV has recently hired two new out-of-town anchormen to replace Bill Beutel, who became host of the ABC network's early morning "A.M. America" show. They work as co-anchormen with Roger Grimsby on the "Eyewitness News" broadcasts at 6 and 11 P.M.

various women's organizations working within the networks themselves.

women's liberation. The national and local attention now focused on the women's movement for equal rights is a controversial issue, particularly in the media. When questioned about the women's liberation movement and its effect on the role of women in television news, most of the women I interviewed expressed support for the movement's goals, especially those of equal opportunity, equal pay, and fair employment practices. The newswomen credited the women's movement with creating a climate of awareness among people and increasing the acceptance of women in the broadcasting profession. Pat Collins expresses her feelings about women's liberation in this way:

> To the extent that they have raised the consciousness level in this country, I approve. To the extent they have gotten very good women with good minds to think about doing something other than doing housework, I approve. To the extent they have been the predominant force behind the Equal Rights Amendment, I approve. To the extent that they want to claim every gain that is made by any woman as their victory, I think that's giving them more credit than they're due. And to the extent that they have made women who do do the housework and do raise children feel less for doing that, I do not approve. . . . I believe in doing what is right for you. I find nothing demeaning at all in raising children. . . . I find bringing along the next generation rather necessary.

Several reporters said the women's movement had had a great personal influence on their lives in terms of better understanding of themselves and their role. Trish Reilly responds with deep introspection and frankness:

> I'm one hundred percent for it and I only wish I were more liberated myself. . . . As a woman who has always had low self-esteem and low confidence, it's very, very hard for me to stand up for myself; for me to fight for my rights; for me to be aggressive and demand what I want. And I've only changed a lot in the last year. And I've found out that you can stand up and fight for what you want and you do get it and people do respect you. You can spend a lifetime sharpening pencils and schlepping coffee and going out and doing the interviews for people, think you're being a good kid, a team player, that some day you'll get your just reward, and in fact you never get it because you've made a doormat of yourself your en-

Trish Reilly, WCBS-TV.

tire life and you get stepped on. I think it's very hard for women to emerge from this pattern. I find it extremely hard. . . . I still haven't made the emotional switch to really believing in myself as much as a lot of men who are half as smart as I am believe in themselves.

Phyllis Haynes offers a different perspective:

I think the women in television news have had a tremendous effect on the movement because they were among the first to break into an all-male environment. We are making a difference. When a woman sits at home and listens to another woman, I think that changes her mind a great deal. I know I was influenced by meeting Liz Trotta, when I was about seventeen years old and had won a scholarship to go to college and Liz Trotta covered the story.[9] Meeting a woman who was telling her crew what to do and shaping a story really might have been my initial motivation to go into broadcasting.

The women in television news who are members of racial and ethnic minorities expressed the belief that the women's liberation movement is "primarily a white middle-class movement." Consequently, they found it difficult to identify themselves with it. Gloria Rojas states her feelings with characteristic candor:

Women's liberation just can't come first when Puerto Rican men have the lowest jobs and get kicked in the face, maybe washing dishes in this restaurant.[10] . . . That's something for a middle-class

9 Phyllis Haynes won a National Merit scholarship from the Ford Foundation upon her graduation from Flushing High School in June 1966.

10 Our interview took place over lunch at Maxwell's Plum, a fashionable restaurant on the east side of New York City.

woman who's educated. . . . I'm not middle class. This middle class is a new thing to me and it doesn't sit that well. I'm a welfare kid. My identification is still with that community. That's why the women's liberation thing, in the sense of marriage and equality, is foreign to me.

Melba Tolliver concurs:

> I feel that it's an important movement, but I feel it's too narrow in its scope for me to be that much involved in it, because I think there ought to be a humanist movement, not a feminist movement. And being black, I can't really be that involved in a movement that's just for women. I have to be concerned about men, women, and children.

Linda Shen tells of her reaction as a Chinese woman:

> At [Channel] 13, there were two groups, a woman's group and a third-world coalition. There were undercurrents in the woman's group that alienated me and when confronted with a choice between the two, I chose first to be a minority and second to be a woman.

Cabell Smith, the first woman network sound technician, worked for NBC on local and network news programs between 1972 and 1974. In speaking of her experiences on the job, she declares:

> At first there was a lot of hostility because of women's lib. . . . These people see women's liberation as taking away their jobs, which are threatened anyway by the tape industry. . . . They see the movement as challenging the family structure, which is ex-

tremely strong in the cultural background these people come from. . . . My answer to that is that I'm an independent person and I need to support myself . . . and I had to be at least as good as most people to get hired. . . . Surprisingly enough, women who could perform their job were accepted with relative ease. Perhaps because a work situation such as this fosters a kind of mutual on-the-job exploring of human relations, and a mutual respect follows for someone who you see, unavoidably, is performing the same tasks as you.

New York City has, undoubtedly, one of the largest and most active women's movements in the country. Within each of the major broadcasting networks a major center of women's rights activity has been created. The broad scope and the variety of these activities have made a significant impact. In February 1973, the Woman's Committee for Equal Employment Opportunity of the National Broadcasting Company filed a formal complaint of across-the-board discrimination because of sex. It was signed by fifty women employees of NBC. The New York City Commission on Human Rights in their January 1975 response found "cause to believe" that the National Broadcasting Company had indeed discriminated against women in recruitment, hiring, job classification, promotion opportunities and benefit programs. The commission's study found that women secretaries at NBC are sex-segregated, have higher qualifications than men in the same jobs, and rarely move to other positions, except to other secretarial jobs.

NBC responded by stating:

The report of the New York City Commission does not find any intentional sex discrimination at NBC, or sex discrimination in any case, and explicitly recognizes that since 1972 NBC has made "measurable

gains" in the employment of women. . . . The commission's report for the years 1967 to 1972 reflects
the historical trends in American society—that
women have been under-utilized in managerial positions and over-utilized in clerical positions. . . .
NBC's affirmative action program has placed particular emphasis on the employment and promotion of
women.

Other legal action involving New York television stations is
still pending. A petition to deny the license renewal of WABC-
TV, brought on behalf of the New York Chapter of the National
Organization of Women (NOW), was filed with the FCC on May
1, 1972. Based on extensive monitoring studies conducted by
NOW, the petition charges massive violations of FCC regulations in that WABC-TV (a) does not consult with women or
women's groups regarding women's programming; (b)
presents a distorted and one-sided image of women; (c) em-
ploys a smaller percentage of women than any other local station. Therefore, the petition argues, WABC-TV is not operating
in the public interest and its license renewal application must
be denied. The FCC found that WABC-TV did not seriously or
systematically discriminate against women. NOW is planning to
appeal this decision in the federal courts.

On September 28, 1972, Elton Rule, ABC President, revised
the network's Equal Employment Opportunity Program to include women: "Women are a most important source of talent
for the company. I expect you to encourage the active and
aggressive recruitment, promotion and advancement of women
at every level within the Broadcast Division."

At CBS, in a policy note from the president dated February
13, 1973, Arthur R. Taylor stated:

Women and men have the same opportunities for
employment and promotion within CBS; there is a

single standard of qualification for employment, and for treatment after employment, for men and women. This is the policy. . . . The attitude of CBS management is that the employment and advancement of women deserves the fullest measure of attention and determination to post results that speak for themselves.

The repercussions of the women's movement have been felt at all levels of the broadcasting hierarchy. The male executives I met with were candid about the effect of the women's liberation movement on their respective organizations. Most of the men admitted to an increased awareness and to the hiring of more newswomen in a positive effort to redress past inequities. Av Westin speaks of the movement's effect:

It's pushed back the walls of restrictions. It has made us all aware that we are surrounded by a group of individuals who have competence or who should be judged more on the basis of competence, rather than ignored because of sex.

Al Primo responds with unreserved frankness:

I think, as a direct result of pressure created by women's liberation, there are more women in television, and people are now looking out to bring women into television. And I think that's a direct result of the pressure. So, you know, this is a country that's been founded on protest. . . . Almost nothing gets accomplished in the United States unless there's a definite protest about it, pressure about it, and [then] it happens. Because basically it is the nature of people not to change anything. . . . I think that women in society have always had a very important role that hasn't been noticed. I don't think that women's liberation is necessarily the thing that has saved women, in the sense that some women don't necessarily need to be saved. I've been married for twelve years, and my wife had a professional career. And we have always shared the burdens of married life. I wash dishes; she washes dishes. I take care of children; she takes care of children. At this particular moment, she's decided that what she wants most to do is be home with the children and function as a housewife. So she's doing that. When she decides to go out and work, I'm sure she'll do just that. . . . I think that women's liberation is probably a great saving device for uneducated people. People who haven't recognized certain intellectual capabilities in anyone around them, or even in themselves, and have just acted out of habit or other role-playing that they've been handed down through the years. . . . I'm Italian. In my family it was generally viewed that women, you know, make a home and raise children and so forth. But it didn't take long to get out into the world and see that that's not necessarily the way it is, or it has to be, or the way you want it. But if I would have never left my original community and worked in my family's business, say, maybe I would have needed the women's liberation movement's jolt to get me to look around at myself and recognize some things that I'd just taken for granted.

Al Ittleson credits the pressures stemming from the women's liberation movement with 90 percent of the improvement recently gained by women in the broadcasting profession:

Women's liberation has been a pain in the ass only because they've been so extreme in some of their views but so right in others. And when they're right and you see they're right, but to change things is such a monumental task in any kind of an organization, the frustration that that creates. . . . They were saying that the population of the country is 53 percent female;[11] therefore, jobs should really be allocated on that basis. That really doesn't make sense, to me anyway. However, they did point up inequities in promotions, inequities in opportunities, and forced us to reconsider what we were doing. Most of the time you do what's convenient, what's easy, what's been done before. But [it was] just that confrontation with reality or reason— . . . The extreme demands didn't do it, but the rational arguments that they presented and that all intelligent people can accept.

Ted Kavenau predicts dire consequences stemming from women's liberation:

As you have an increase in these minorities that were traditionally held down, as their roles change and, as we accept them and bring them in, that is an index to the decline and destruction of the society. . . . I consider when women enter into what basically are masculine fields, not so much through competence, but through demands based upon sex equality, that it's the beginning of an imminent collapse. . . . When you have to hire by quotas, it's a destructive fact. Now, it's a reality, but it's the end.

11 On April 1, 1970, women made up 51.3 percent of the population of the United States (104,299,734 women in the total population). U.S. Department of Commerce, Bureau of the Census, *We the American Women* (Washington, D.C.: U.S. Government Printing Office, 1973), p. 2.

Male broadcasting executives, reflecting cultural expectations about the appropriateness of woman's role, believe that women are unable to represent authority: "The notion of a pretty young woman announcing a revolution or a sudden death is regarded as highly inappropriate." [12] From the early years of radio, the male voice has dominated the airwaves. Audiences have been thoroughly conditioned to accept and to believe in the male newscaster. Long-held attitudes rooted in our culture do not easily change. Yet, unquestionably, exposure to women correspondents who are highly competent will lead to complete acceptance. Television is the country's most powerful force in the shaping of people's attitudes. The appearance of qualified women in greater numbers on television will lead to the disappearance of credibility doubts and to the redefinition of woman's role in broadcasting.

12 Norman Swallow, *Factual Television* (London: Focal Press, 1966), p. 32.

5
double
tokenism

Racial and ethnic factors are crucial considerations in the television medium and affect career opportunity and attainment. An analysis of 30 newswomen according to racial and ethnic background shows that 20 (66.6 percent) are white; 7 (23.3 percent) are black; 2 (6.6 percent) are oriental; and 1 (3.3 percent) is Puerto Rican. Therefore, one-third of the women in the limited sample are members of racial minorities.

On a national basis, full-time employment of minority personnel at commercial television stations increased from 8 percent of the work force in 1971 to 12 percent in 1974. The 613 commercial stations included in a study of employment practices compiled by the Office of Communications of the United Church of Christ indicated that of new employees added between 1971 and 1974, 72 percent were members of minority groups, while new women employees made up 58 percent of the total.[1] These two categories overlap, since some new employees are female members of minorities. While these statistics are regarded as encouraging, they are not an accidental occurrence. A concerted effort to rectify group injustices has resulted in the widespread practice of hiring a woman who is also a member of a racial minority and thereby creating the stigma of double tokenism. Maureen Bunyan expresses her reaction to the existence of such tokenism:

> There's an old saying that black newswomen have always been a double token. Well, I think that's probably true in many places. I would say I was hired partially because I'm black. There's no doubt about that. Numbers are very important. And partially because I'm a woman. If you see the staff, you see the ratio, the number of women to men. You see the ratio of black to white. And that's been true everywhere I've ever worked. I've never worked under the illusion that my blackness or my femininity doesn't have anything to do with my getting a job. I would say it probably has helped me because it has made me a salable commodity. I'm in demand. I was in demand. Ten years ago it would have been a totally different story. I would have been out in left field. In other words, I wouldn't have gotten a job as a woman or as a black person.

Theresa Brown is equally candid in her response:

> It's very difficult when you're black to figure out when you don't get the job whether or not it's because you're a woman and you're black. When you

1 Ralph M. Jennings and David A. Tillyer, *Television Station Employment Practices: The Status of Minorities and Women* (New York: Office of Communications, United Church of Christ, 1973), p. 2.

get the job, everybody automatically assumes it's because you're a woman and you're black. Now, in your own mind you can't really know because you can never tell, especially what's in a white person's mind. You have absolutely no concept of what they're thinking, and their true feelings are never going to come out to you in a job interview. Now, when you do get a job everybody says, "Well, they wanted a black woman," which necessarily puts you on a level where you have to prove yourself above being a woman and being black. . . . Now, I would say, in certain situations, it helped me simply because I was mildly attractive, not because I was black or a woman. That gets you more mileage than anything else. And I would say that's above being black. . . . God help you if you're not an attractive woman. And I'm not hysterically attractive, but I'm attractive enough to get by. . . .

Judy Thomas describes the difficulties created by tokenism:

You have to prove that you're qualified to everybody. Most people tend to assume that you're hired because you're black and because you're a woman and because they were desperate. Not because you know what you're doing. . . . Years ago neither women nor blacks were allowed on television, point blank. Now that we're allowed, it's like they're looking for "qualified" women, "qualified" minorities. And I think the reason I got my job is because they were looking for qualified minorities and women— the combination.

Phyllis Haynes feels no role discomfort as a black woman in television:

>That's something that I've been very touchy about. There is a great deal of tokenism in the minds of management in various television shops. But the fact is, and this I say without a doubt, that most of the black people who are still on the air, who are working full time, would have been hired whether they were black or white. Those that were hired as tokens don't make it. They fall out. They fail.

Phyllis Haynes is confident that she would have been hired for the same television jobs whether or not she was black:

>Yes, if I were a white woman or a white male. But that's because I believe in what I'm doing and I'm speaking for myself. I happen to be very happy being what I am and I don't wear it as a shield. I don't let it get in the way of my reporting. If I happen to see something abominable in the black community caused by blacks, I'll say it as well as I would about anything in the white community. . . . In ["Straight Talk"] obviously there is an important relationship between me and Elie [Guggenheimer] [2] in that I'm black and was raised in Bedford-Stuyvesant and Elie is a white Jewish woman who is very active in the political structure in our city. I think that relationship makes the show very interesting, and because I am black, I can speak from a different experiential situation.

Norma Quarles entered the television profession "when it was a fortuitous time for black women." Now she believes she represents "all things to all men":

[2] Mary Helen McPhillips has replaced Elinor Guggenheimer on "Straight Talk." Mary Helen is white and Roman Catholic.

Norma Quarles, WNBC-TV "Newscenter 4."

The funny thing is, the public is very strange. If they take a liking to a television personality, they will give that person whatever role or whatever they choose to make. So that I have people in the audience that swear up and down I'm Chinese. In Cleveland I once received a call from a Ukranian to do an interview, "We want you to do the interview because we Ukranians are not exactly white and you're not exactly white either." . . . There's a kind of *sympatico* with Puerto Ricans. It's just very strange.

Often the firing of a minority person presents as complex a situation as the original hiring. The attrition rate for blacks is high in broadcasting. There are not too many black men who have survived well in this profession. Racism is not always the cause of dismissal. Carol Jenkins explains:

> Most stations have so few reporters and have so many stories to cover that they really can't afford to hire people who can't go into any situation. . . . If you're sent into these situations and you can't handle them, then in very short order you find yourself not handling them. It's just a matter then of talent. What happens very often in this business is that people say, "Well, because I'm black, they didn't hire me [or] they fired me"; or "Because I'm a woman they didn't hire me [or] they fired me." I think in many cases it's not having prior experience and not being able to handle the situation. . . . What keeps this business moving and thriving nine times out of ten is the fear of being trampled upon. So you move, you run. You develop your skills in this business or you're out. There's no such thing as resting for a week or a month, because you're on your way out. And it's a turntable. It's a revolving door. But, again, that's the nature of the business and not any particular persecution.

A black male reporter speaks of a minority firing at his station:

> If X hadn't been black, he'd have been canned long before this. He was incompetent and he was nasty. The real racism lay in hiring him, not firing him. They wanted a token, and they grabbed a black face without regard for competence. I think it's a

sign of diminishing racism that they're getting up the nerve to fire an incompetent black.[3]

When suddenly people are hired without regard to their background and experience, but solely on the basis of racial or ethnic factors, they are forced to work harder under difficult and psychologically damaging circumstances to prove their worth as individuals both to themselves and to their colleagues. Token and quota hiring express contempt for the ability of the black or the woman to compete in the professional world on an equal basis. Ted Kavenau comments on the problem:

> I think that it's true, if you get to a white middle-class world, that if you're black or Puerto Rican or a woman, you've got to be twice as good to be really taken seriously [and not] taken as a token.

Pat Collins talks of the residual effect of token hiring:

> Every time there is a woman hired by a station, and I won't go into names, for reasons other than her competence, or potential competency, she does us—I speak of women collectively in broadcasting—a great disservice. . . . She, in some ways, is an embarrassment. That sets us back enormously . . . with the viewership and her cohorts and with management. They tend, because it's human nature, to talk about the bad people. . . . Taking someone off the street who's never done television before and putting her on the air, just to fill a certain need, because she

3 Quoted in Edith Efron, "What Is Happening to Blacks in Broadcasting?" *TV Guide,* August 19, 1972, p. 22.

looks pretty or whatever. . . . We won't be advanced much.

Gabe Pressman, one of the very best and most dedicated newsmen in the profession, reflects on token hiring:

> Women can be as competent as men. The problem is when women are hired as tokens instead of for competence. This is the fault of the boobs who do the hiring and are unable to recognize different levels of competence—their inability to choose a competent journalist rather than a body!

Chris Borgen is another dedicated journalist who is profoundly disturbed by current hiring practices. He describes the audition of twenty-five different women for the job of on-air reporter, "all cosmetic types without any background in news":

> They began to hire the "broad," the "face," the "body," and in the rush the women who were hired for the wrong reasons left no room for the qualified ones who were around—and what does that make of us? If anyone, barmaids and models, can come in as a reporter, we are no profession at all!

Roger Grimsby concurs:

> Well, [token hiring takes place] because of the panic situation on the part of management, "Got to get a girl, got to get an Italian, got to get a Puerto Rican, got to get a black." And they do it under pressure and they do it too soon, too fast. And it's a disservice both to the station and to the person who is hired. In my opinion, however, it is a transition that we're all going to have to go through.

Rose Ann Scamardella admits to being hired as a "rookie reporter" mainly because of ethnic considerations:

> From what I understand, I think they were looking for a woman. They were looking for an ethnic woman, an Italian woman. They had no Italian reporter. That probably gave me an in. The same way it did Geraldo [Rivera] as a Puerto Rican and Melba [Tolliver] as a black woman. None of us had journalistic experience before we came here. . . . Rather than a seasoned journalist—they have a lot of them—they were looking more for a street-people kind of person.

Connie Chung believes that being an oriental woman has helped her in the television news world because she is "different." Although she definitely stands out from the crowd, after the initial reaction she is hopeful that the viewer will "relax and just listen and pay attention to what I have to say."

Linda Shen is more outspoken about the effect of her ethnic background on her advancement within the television profession:

> I was hired specifically because I was a third-world woman. But I think that had a lot to do with my being let go as a matter of fact, so it's a double-edged sword. . . . I, as a Chinese woman, was far more expendable than either a black or a Spanish woman. . . . The Asian community is not a large community in New York and it certainly is not a community that plays New York politics. It's a very quiet community. . . . I have been labeled by the news director's office as a radical young upstart, a troublemaker. Those were his words, and that I was a thorn in the side of the news director. One of those things

has to do with the fact that I have complained about assignments that I thought were either unjust or just set up in unworkable fashion. . . . As one example, I was assigned to do a story on Thanksgiving Day, on a Chinese Thanksgiving. There's no such thing as a Chinese Thanksgiving. . . . "You're just exploiting my people. I'll do the story as it has to be done." . . . I believe there are different expectations of me, not only because I'm female, but because I'm a minority female.

Gloria Rojas is the only Puerto Rican news reporter in our group of newswomen. She became the first Hispanic employed by a New York television station when she joined WCBS-TV. Gloria was one of the original two women and eighteen men selected for the Columbia University School of Journalism's program for minorities when it began in 1968: [4] "I was probably one of the few Puerto Ricans to even apply. So, I guess that if there's any tokenism involved, it was the Puerto Rican angle rather than the woman angle." She feels that she personally owes a debt of responsibility to the Puerto Rican community:

I'm where I am because I'm Puerto Rican. There aren't that many of us. Let me give you an example. My son, in an elementary school, did not want to be Puerto Rican because the kids were grouped hetero-geneously and he knew that the smart kids were the white, Jewish kids in his class, and the dumb kids were the black, Puerto Rican kids. Well, he's half Jewish and half Puerto Rican. So until he was in third grade, he'd never say that he was Puerto Rican. So he would say he was Jewish. Herman Badillo came to our school to talk and all of a sudden my kid

4 The Ford Foundation concluded support for this program in 1974.

became a Puerto Rican. All of a sudden he saw it isn't just being the dumb kids. It has more. I think that's what I do for Puerto Ricans. . . . When I go to talk, people see that I'm not so sensational and they might say, "I can do that too." . . . It's absolutely more important for people to identify with me as a Puerto Rican rather than as a woman.

Photo: Elizabeth Gee

Gloria Rojas, WABC-TV "Eyewitness News."

The men in management expressed differing opinions when questioned about the existence of ethnic factors in their hiring practices. Of those men who refused to admit that ethnic considerations affected their choice of news reporters, several did modify their response by speaking of the need for a balanced news presentation. Robert Mulholland says:

> We still hire reporters, period. But the government encourages you to make sure that you have a cross-section on your staff. If it so turned out, the way the staff had worked around, that we were all white and all male, and we had an opening, I think that I'd probably, everything else being equal, I'd tend to vary the staff.

Al Primo does not believe the ethnic factors are a significant determinative:

> I think that we tend to overemphasize that, in the sense that some of the minority people that we have hired have demonstrated some fantastic ability as reporters, which is a real indication of the potential available for all those years that wasn't tapped or used. Geraldo Rivera could be a woman, could be a WASP, could be a black, could be anything and would probably be just as outstanding as he is at the moment. The fact that he is Puerto Rican enabled him to come into television news without ten years' experience and as an anchorman. But he certainly was an investment that was fantastic because he's really helping people and he's reporting and he's bringing to our station a great image that we are concerned about. We want representation and we're getting it.

Many of the men I spoke with openly admitted to feeling the pressures to hire and train minority employees and to increase the complement of minorities on their respective staffs. Most say that they respond affirmatively to the obligation to look more carefully for minority group people and to recognize and encourage their advancement. All stations are involved in a conscious effort toward an ethnic balance. Al Ittelson explains:

I think you pick people to fill certain slots and I think, yeah, you have to take race and ethnic background into consideration, because the people we're talking to out there don't consider themselves just people. They also consider themselves Italians or blacks or Jews and they relate to people we have on the air. That's why the blacks push for black newscasters, so that their children would have someone to believe in, along with giving their side of the story as well. Because white reporters were not quite as sensitive to the black issues as black reporters. But the important thing to me, anyway, is that people sitting at home can look at the set and see themselves.

One news director is troubled by current trends:

Television is subject to government control. Every three years they review the license. Every three years they go through a file, which I find demeaning both to me and to the people I hire. It's called an Affirmative Action Report and I list how many minority groups, Spanish surnamed, are working for me. Every month I turn one of these in and my point is that I don't hire these people because of their surnames or their race or their sex. . . . When television started, there were all sorts of prejudices against blacks, Spaniards, women. Now I think, the pendulum has swung. They're trying very, very hard to hire these people and a great many times leap-frogging qualified people that have been in in order to open opportunity. I don't know whether this is right or wrong. I don't think you can ever make up for past history.

The increase of minority personnel in the broadcasting profession is a pressured effort to redress past prejudicial practices. The inclusion of members of all population groups will serve to broaden the cultural diversity of the television medium as well as introducing new attitudes, new values, and new perceptions. In the long run, a racial and ethnic balance will prove beneficial both to the television stations themselves and to the audiences they serve.

6
career versus
home life

Most women in television news have relinquished traditional roles in seeking and attaining a professional career. More than three-quarters of our group of television news-women were unmarried at the time of their interview. Sixteen (53.5 percent) were single and never married; 7 (23.3 percent) were divorced; and 7 were married. Of the 7 married women, 3 had been married previously and divorced prior to remarriage. Among the 7 divorced women, 3 had children at home from their earlier marriages. There was a total of 12 children (2 adopted) among the group of 30 women included in this study.

All the single women I spoke with were united in the belief that marriage would have substantially altered their careers and their professional advancement. An on-air newscaster's job requires all the time, all the energy, and all the effort a woman possesses; there is little left over for personal life or commitments. Most of the women also found it necessary to travel all over the country in the course of their careers. Such mobility is difficult, if not impossible, with family obligations. The newswomen, when they do manage the time for social dating, make it a conscious policy to look for and date men who share their ideas about life-style and sexual roles. For the majority of single newswomen, marriage and children are not a viable option. With no responsibility except to themselves and to their careers, the women I interviewed never were faced with the conflict imposed by dual role demands and never were forced to limit their career potential or aspirations. Yet few would totally rule out the possibility of marriage at some future point in their lives. Maureen Bunyan comments:

> This has been a very demanding career both time-wise and physically and emotionally, too. I am ambitious and I'm dedicated and I know how much that takes out of me. Say I'd gotten married five or six years ago, before I'd really gotten into this. I think it would have been very difficult for the marriage to sustain itself because I have worked incredible hours. I have moved. I have lived in three different cities in three different years. Basically, I just want to do what I feel like doing, and I still want to continue doing that. I would like, eventually, to settle down in one way or another because I think that is very important, too. I'm not a loner. I need attention. I need love just as much as everyone else does.

Pat Collins reflects on her choice:

> I have been engaged twice and in both instances, as I think about those fellows and our situation, I would be a divorced mother of four now, struggling, trying maybe either to get into this business or to

stay in it. My kids would hate me. . . . Looking back, it would have been absolute disaster for everybody.

Several single women expressed the need for a complete and deep relationship with a man without, necessarily, the traditional ties of marriage. Such freedom allows the woman an opportunity to have "my life as well as our life." Melba Tolliver, who was divorced several years ago "because we didn't get along," is single today but feels a close relationship is important in life:

> The thing about being single or not having any big romance in your life is that your work becomes the most important thing in your life. I don't want my work to be that way. It is now, because it is the biggest ongoing thing in my life. But if I were married, I'd hope I'd have a much more relaxed approach to work.

The women who were divorced but had the responsibility of caring for children definitely felt the additional burden imposed by motherhood. This duality resulted in personal conflict and feelings of guilt.

Norma Quarles is divorced with two children, a son 17 years old and a daughter 13 years old. They live in their own four-bedroom house in Mount Vernon, New York. She describes the problem:

> In my own case I also have another life. I have a home life. I have children. I have a house. I have chores that have to be done. I have two jobs. I have one at work and one at home. They both have to be taken care of and there just is not enough time to do both. So something has to be sacrificed. I think that my home life suffers and that my children suffer be-

cause of the hours in this business, and that's a disadvantage. Let's take last Christmas. I got beautiful Christmas cards from my co-workers, male co-workers. Who sent out the Christmas cards? Their wives! I have no one at home sending out Christmas cards for me. I've absolutely no time. You work twelve to fourteen hours. There's not time to sit and write out Christmas cards. The weekend is packed with the chores, so I haven't gotten cards out in two years.

Norma Quarles also feels that her family obligations have limited her career aspirations:

I have never really pitched for a network assignment [1] job because it involves traveling all over the country, all over the world. And as a mother with the responsibility of children, I really can't do that. Yet it would be an upgrade both financially and professionally.

Gloria Rojas has a teen-aged son from an early marriage that ended in divorce. She has been faced with the need to balance her career commitment with the responsibility she has to her child:

When I worked in the newsroom [WCBS-TV], I worked Saturdays. It's fair. I mean everybody has to take their turn on Saturdays and Sundays because the news has to get covered and the news has to go on. . . . That's one of the things about being a woman. You know, a man, if he's got kids, well, his

1 Network assignments involve national news coverage as opposed to local news stories.

wife is home taking care of them. She can make the graduation. . . . But when you're a parent and if that's your job and there isn't anybody else, it gets very trying at times.

Virginia Sherwood was married for nineteen years and had three children, two boys and a girl. She speaks of her own alternatives at various points in her life:

> I always put my family and children first. . . . I never moved anywhere. I never tried to. As long as I was married and my children were small, I stayed with them. . . . I never tried to move up in television or try for anything more until after I was separated.

None of the women who were divorced felt that her career was a cause of any disharmony with her partner. Most of these women began their television careers after the dissolution of their marriages. Several newswomen said that they found satisfaction in working because of their unhappiness in marriage.

Pauline Frederick was married for the first time in 1969.[2] Although she now says marriage is "wonderful; if I had known it was so great I would have done it long ago," she also states that an earlier marriage would have made a difference in her career:

> My situation is quite different from other women who have had children or who have come into their career in an earlier stage in their marriage. I think with the kind of career I've had, something would have had to be sacrificed. Because when I have been busy at the United Nations during crises, it has

2 Pauline Frederick is married to Charles Robbins, who is the President of the Atomic Industrial Forum and former managing editor of the *Wall Street Journal*.

meant working day and night. You can't very well take care of a home when you do something like that, or children.

Pia Lindstrom was recently married for the second time. She was first married in 1960 during her senior year at Mills College in Oakland, California, and divorced eighteen months later. She says, "I've been single most of my life. I was hardly married. I got married at twenty and divorced at twenty-one." In 1971, she married Joseph Daly, a mortgage broker and they now have 2 young sons.[3]

Pia feels that her career is no longer the only thing that matters in her life and she would like to alter her work schedule. When questioned about her husband's attitude toward the necessity of working odd hours in television news, she replied:

> That's going to be a problem. How could he possibly like it if I get put back on the one o'clock news and don't come home until one-thirty at night? I just can't accept those kinds of jobs. The only thing I can hope is that I've already made my reputation to such a degree that I'll be able to say I don't want to work those hours. But you can't go to work somewhere and then say, "Well, gee, I only work days," because nobody only works days. When you start you do whatever you have to do. And if they tell you to work nights, you work the night shift. . . . Now, I'm hoping, I have put in seven years of that stuff. . . . Now I hope on my next job I can say I only want to work three days a week, or I only want to work a few hours a day, or I only want to work weekends because now the child, in a sense, is more important. I was going

3 At the time of our interview, Pia was still on maternity leave after the birth of her first son, Justin Christopher. The baby was cradled in her arms as she responded to these questions.

Pia Lindstrom, WNBC-TV "Newscenter 4."

to say "as" important but that doesn't sound right, does it?

Pia Lindstrom is making a conscious effort to integrate her growing family and her career responsibilities. She appeared on "Newscenter 4" one day wearing a black top with the word "BABY" outlined in sequins together with an arrow pointing downward. She explained that many viewers had written asking "why I'm dressing so matronly? Well, I'm going to be a matron!" Pia was then seven months pregnant with her second child and stated on the air, "I didn't want them to think I'm just fat." [4] A film crew was one of the early visitors to the New York Hospital bedside of Pia and her second son as he made his initial television appearance by the side of his mother. Her professionalism during pregnancy did not go unnoticed. Before the birth of her first child Pia also worked until the very last days. A cameraman who worked with her quite often then told me admiringly: "Two weeks before the delivery of her baby, Pia walked up five flights of stairs and carried my small camera too!"

Barbara Walters was first married following her graduation from Sarah Lawrence College, but the marriage was annulled after a year. She was remarried for more than 10 years to Lee Gruber,[5] a theatrical producer. She lives in Manhattan with her 6-year-old daughter, Jacqueline. Barbara Walters does not think that a successful career in television news can be combined with a successful marriage and a family:

> I have a child. I would not want to be a correspondent. I could not travel all over the country at this point in my life. And when I was traveling all over the country, I wasn't married. I think there are choices you have to make, in this field more than any other. And if you want to have a marvelous social life and go out at night, even have a pretty decent social life, you can't do it with this job and you certainly can't be married. . . . My child was born when I was in my late thirties. I already had this job when she was born. If I had had my child and husband then

4 WNBC-TV, January 20, 1975.

5 At the time of our interview, the Grubers were in the midst of a temporary separation.

[earlier in her career], I'm not sure I could have gone all over the country doing stories. And it still is difficult when I go away. I'm rarely away for more than a week or ten days at a time. I have extremely good help. I can literally go to China and not worry about my child. That costs money. You have to be able to make enough money to have this kind of a person. And, then, I'm always somewhat torn between my child and the job. . . . I think if you want to do this, you have to wait until you're somewhat established. And you can't do it with a young child at home. You cannot arrange your hours if you're going to be in the news business. And when you speak to the men in the news business, what they say most is, they're away so much it breaks up their marriages. They don't see their kids. There are too many divorces going on in the news business because you're traveling. . . . I think everything in life is a choice. You can't have it all. . . . It's part of the job. And if you want this job, man or woman, then you decide what your priorities are. . . . No management is forcing you to become a news correspondent.

At the conclusion of our interview, Barbara Walters asked me the ages of my own children. When I told her, she replied: "How do you do it? I'm constantly torn. My daughter says, 'Oh Mommy, are you going to work again?'" There was no comment I could make that would make it easier the next time, for either of us.

Helen Marmor [6] has been with NBC News for twenty years. She believes that the work is so demanding that men and women in the field find it necessary to sacrifice everything to their job:

6 Helen Marmor is divorced. She has no children.

> There are many men, and I work right near them, who devote twelve hours a day to their jobs. . . . I think it's an economic arrangement. The women run the home for them and raise the children and they pop in from time to time and change their laundry. They're career men.

The only woman in our group who has successfully managed over the years to combine a career in television with marriage and a family is Marlene Sanders. She has been married for seventeen years to Jerome Toobin, a producer for public television. They have two children. Outside of minor inconveniences, she has never felt hampered in her career because of her family commitments, nor has she ever felt guilty about her professional obligations and her inability to be a full-time mother at home. Her husband is very supportive of her goals: "He's been a big booster. He always wants me to get a better job, to advance. He thinks I'm talented. Every time I have a bad break, he's ready to storm. He's terrific." Her 15-year-old son, Jeff, accepts her dual role completely:

> He doesn't know any other situation, and the kind of work I do is particularly interesting. When he was in the first or second grade, his class visited my studio. He always knew what I was doing and he has been on film assignments with me. He's very interested in news, probably the best informed kid in the class [laugh] and he finds it very interesting. I think there were times when he probably didn't want me to be away, but it was probably good for him. He's really an independent child, not overprotected. He gets a lot of attention when I'm around. It's a qualitative kind and I feel, and the stories I've done on the subject and the people I've talked to— The kids whose mothers are hovering around and may be frustrated

and resentful—I haven't noticed those kids are any better off. He did say to me a few years ago . . . when he began to be aware of other kinds of households that existed. . . . He said, "So and so's mother doesn't work. What does she do around the house all day? She must be very bored." He couldn't conceive of what a mother did at home all day. . . . I hope he doesn't grow up resenting it. I have no indication that he does. . . . I really have *never* felt guilty.

Once or twice a typical childhood problem arose in her household, during one of her absences. Her son contracted the mumps while she was overseas in Vietnam. She tells of receiving a letter with the news from her husband, who later accused her of being unsympathetic in her reply:

But I knew by the time he got the letter, the mumps would be finished. We had help. My mother came in and it passed all right. I felt badly about not being there, but everybody handled it very well. My husband also had to cope with the measles during my absence. In fact, Jeff now says to me when I go away on a shooting assignment, he says, "Well, chickenpox is on schedule at some point." He hasn't gotten that yet. But everybody managed.

In the television news profession, those women who are able to manage a full-time career commitment and to capably fulfill their responsibilities to a husband and children remain relative rarities. It takes exceptional skill, organizational ability, determination, and luck to combine harmoniously a family life and such a demanding career. Even in a society in which the man's career role is the dominant one, male newscasters also have had great difficulty in maintaining a satisfactory home life. Happy marriages among professional newsmen are not common. Gabe Pressman, for seventeen years a top New York reporter with WNBC-TV and currently with WNEW-TV, declares: "I've seen marriage after marriage crumble because hours are so demanding and because there is so little time left for home life. My job was 90 percent of my life. Today it's 80 percent."

Betsy Aaron is herself a widow. She expresses strong feelings about the difficulties inherent in maintaining a working marriage in this field:

> I can't think of any worse business than this one to try to manage a successful marriage. It's the worst. It's the same for the men. No one has a successful marriage in this business that I know. They work seven days a week and never see their family. I just don't understand that kind of marriage.

The majority of newswomen have made a conscious choice of a career. Nonmarriage leaves them enough emotional energy and physical time to succeed at their respective careers. Several women told me they had decided not to have any children of their own. Phyllis Haynes said: "I don't want any children. If I do have children I will adopt them. I believe in zero population growth." As the climate of opinion slowly begins turning against the traditional idea that homemaking can be the only form of achievement open to women, different options and more flexible life-styles will allow women to realize their potential and will enrich their individual lives.

A world that does not discriminate on the basis of sex would enable women and men to seek any life-style at any time in their lives. No longer would women be forced into a role that they may or may not be suited for. A woman would be free of guilt and self-consciousness if she does not choose to bear children. Conversely, a woman would be free to choose the traditional roles of wife or mother, not because she is unaware or incapable of other roles, but because these give her the greatest satisfaction. The sense of freedom that comes through a conscious choice among viable options is the essential ingredient. If the woman then chooses to stay at home, she is doing it because she wants to and not from an inarticulate sense of being trapped. The difference is between taking a long mountain hike to enjoy the outdoors and taking a long hike because over the mountain lies survival. The rebirth of feminism in America has raised serious questions about the way people live—about their families, home, child rearing, jobs, and the nature of the sexes themselves.

Many of our newswomen are personally pointing the evolutionary way toward societal reorganization. As Margaret Mead writes:

> The problems facing articulate, educated women remain as vivid today as they have been throughout European history. The continuous care given to small children, a husband, and a household usually is incompatible with the singleminded pursuit of a career. The life style of the good wife and mother contrasts sharply with that of the good scientist, artist, or executive. . . . A woman's life as a homemaker need not be opposed to her individual self-realization, with the one treated as a noble duty and the other as selfish and self-seeking. . . . Society must also support fully women's right to remain unmarried, their right to a personal life without children, to a career alone or to a life of devotion to a small circle of others.[7]

7 Margaret Mead, "Epilogue," in Margaret Mead and Francis B. Kaplan, eds., *American Women: The Report of the President's Commission on the Status of Women and Other Publications of the Commission* (New York: Scribner's, 1965), pp. 201–4.

7
career guidance and advice

The growing prominence of women in television news has made the profession appear increasingly attractive to young women who are planning for future careers. While the acceptance of women as television reporters can be expected to continue, it is important that those who intend to prepare themselves for this kind of career do so intelligently, with an adequate knowledge of the realities of the profession. The women I interviewed repeatedly emphasized the fact that often people are drawn into the television news world by a false idea of glamour, only to find out their mistake too late. Rebecca Bell warns: "If anybody is misled enough to get into this field for glamour, or for money, or excitement, they're in for a hell of a disappointment. Those things are there, but they're only minor things." Theresa Brown agrees that a false sense of glamour surrounds her job:

I know several women now who would give their legs, arms, teeth, and brain to be in television news primarily because they think it is a glamour job. Now, I personally don't think there's anything glamorous about it. . . . It's a pain in the neck to always worry about how you look, and to run around combing your hair and touching up your makeup. And you feel this is totally incongruous with your role as a reporter but it's very important before you go on camera. . . . But the most important thing is to want it very much . . . because perseverance is it above all.

Judy Thomas believes her career requires total commitment:

It's an awful sacrifice in terms of your health and welfare. You have to be awfully committed. It has to be a little like cigarettes, some sort of addiction, otherwise you can't get through the bad parts. . . . The stamina and the feelings of insecurity and all the tensions. . . .

All the newswomen spoke of the need for perseverance and determination in those who aspire to a broadcasting career. It is necessary, first, to want to do it very much and, second, to be willing to pay the price it requires. Marlene Sanders explains:

They have to recognize that it's a long road. That they have to work irregular hours and put in a long period of time before they can expect to get the job they think they want now. That if they get into news, they may have to work the assignment desk from midnight to 8 A.M. for six months to a year. And this is a terrible shift. And a lot of the things you have to do are unpleasant. There is an aura of glamour which is false. You do get to meet important, famous,

Photo: Curtis Brown, Ltd.

Marlene Sanders, ABC News, in Vietnam

accomplished people part of the time. The rest of the time it's hard work. They have to be persistent. They have to be prepared.

For women looking for jobs in television news, there is no single beaten path, only some indirect routes. Barbara Walters describes the two most commonly accepted patterns:

There are two points of view: one is to get your foot in the door and to get in any way you can. . . . The other way is, by all means don't start off as a secretary. Have them accept you as a news reporter. I really don't know which is best. On our program, almost everybody, our writers and so forth, started out as secretaries or even receptionists and then became production assistants. So, I guess, the best thing I could say is just get in there somehow. Work very hard. Learn how to write. Learn your craft and do as much writing as you can. Learn how to do film. Listen and learn. Don't think you know it all, and realize that you have to make choices about your personal life.

Pia Lindstrom suggests a more detailed job pattern:

I'd start with my school newspaper and go to my local town newspaper, wherever that is, and get a job doing everything and anything and do that for a year. And then you can go somewhere and say, "I've already worked for the *Arkansas Express* and now I'm ready for Columbus, Ohio." And move around. Go from city to city. The television station is much more impressed with a lot of jobs than, say, "For the last ten years I've been working on my Ph.D. and I've had one job for five years as a copy girl." That's no good.

But if you say, "I've had fifteen jobs" . . . that shows more versatility and that's what they want. Lots of little things that you've been able to do. And go to a local radio station. Get a job doing anything. To begin with, you have to just get your foot in the door. . . . I wouldn't be picky about what I want to do at the beginning—anything, just to get in there, because once you're in there you can see what the possibilities are, or you can go to another station and say, "Listen, I've already worked at one station." You don't have to be too specific about what you did, nobody is. They list their credits, you know. They don't necessarily say, "I brought the coffee." They say, I was an assistant to whoever it was. That will be O.K. They won't know and that's seriously the way to get a job. I've seen people come in with reports you wouldn't believe and they've been fired from these jobs. And they don't even say that they've been fired and the reason they've had ten jobs is because they've been fired from each of them. They walk in and the news director says, "Look at the list of credits where this person has been," you know. Someone else can come in. They've just been in one place, steady employment, and it doesn't look as good.

While there is not complete agreement on what level is the best to start a television news career, most of our correspondents were agreed that New York City is not the right place to begin a career in broadcasting. Marjorie Margolies states with strong conviction:

Don't do it in New York. Come to New York with a lot of credentials, because if you come to New York and you start as a researcher, you can stay there for twenty years. Go to a small city and get all the credentials you can possibly get. Do all the press conferences you can possibly do and then come to New York with a good résumé saying, "Look what I've done." That's the only way you can get a good job.

The right preparation is essential for those who plan to enter television news. Melba Tolliver offers this advice:

The thing that disturbs me about some of the letters I get, and I understand it because I didn't come along the traditional route, is that a lot of people think that they're just going to come into a place and go on the air and,I mean, that doesn't happen for men and it doesn't happen for women either. I've been one of the different ones. I don't consider myself lucky because I had to come into a job and make a lot of mistakes where everybody could watch. And that wasn't a very good feeling. I would much have preferred to work for a wire service, to work for a small station out of town, and come to New York. It gives you a great deal of security because you know you've gone through all these steps—for me, because that's my personality. I get very discouraged when people say, "Well, I don't want to go out of town. I don't want to work for a wire service." Well, damn it, if you want to do it, you'll do anything that you think is going to lead you in that direction. You'll work for a wire service. You'll work for a small station. You won't come out of journalism school and think that you know it all and that you can just walk in.

Sara Pentz specifically outlines the dedicated preparation she feels is necessary for a successful television career:

You should be sitting in front of your mirror at least two hours practicing and rehearsing into a tape recorder, writing news shows, doing copy. Sitting there working at it, slaving at it. There's no excuse for your not doing that. When I practiced, when I worked at this for ten months, I did that every day. I wrote copy. I wrote news shows. I took my tape recorder; I tape recorded Nancy Dickerson [1] off the television set. I transcribed; I rewrote it. I read it. I compared my voice to hers. I did everything. I tried to learn style but kept my style at the same time. I did it with men. I did it with all the women I could find on television. I then went to the Yellow Pages and found myself a closed-circuit television school that I could go to. . . . You must be very good and hard working at it. You'll always be rewarded because people in high positions are always looking for talented, creative, good, hard-working people. And don't anybody tell me that isn't true, because if you tell me that isn't true, it means you're not working hard enough.

Virginia Sherwood suggests the following preparation for a career in television news:

I think the best thing to do, first of all, is to get an education and not to jump out of high school and to think, "Oh, I want to go into television news," and serving an apprenticeship and being a mail girl or a desk assistant or something like that. Working your way up the ranks is fine, that's one thing. But I think when you get to be a correspondent, you need the background. And I don't think just a journalism back-

1 Nancy Dickerson became the first woman television correspondent for CBS in February 1960. She later joined NBC and currently has her own syndicated minute-and-a-half news program, which she calls "Columns of News."

ground. I think the best correspondents have done many things. . . . I think a good liberal-arts background and some study of journalism, and then don't expect to go to the top immediately. I'm always amused by people who've never worked at a local station anywhere. They've never worked a desk. They've never done any film editing themselves or worked with a film editor and they want to be a network correspondent. I think you have to be willing to serve your time. That's not a prejudice against women. Every man reporter I know has served some time learning somewhere.

Young women who plan a broadcasting career should not expect to be able to have doors swing open wider for them because of their membership in the female sex. Gloria Rojas states emphatically:

Don't expect to get handed something because you're a woman, because that time is over. The time of hiring women and blacks who aren't qualified and feeling you couldn't fire them, that's over. You've got to be willing to take your lumps and stop yelling discrimination every time somebody doesn't make it. . . . Less and less that's an excuse. If you really are good, you gotta get up. Ability is as visible in women now as it is in men. . . . With very few exceptions, the women who are in the business have paid their dues.

As women are now being accepted into most television news jobs, the men I spoke with indicated a belief that women are in the broadcasting profession to stay. Today, young women are able to prepare themselves for a career in television news with the full knowledge that there will be jobs open to

Virginia Sherwood, formerly ABC News.

them. But they must first take the time to become good journalists. Stan Opotowsky enumerates the preparatory steps to enter television news:

> Not as women, as persons who want to go into broadcasting, first get the education, which is best a two-pronged education: one, general, with the emphasis on economics, political science, various other areas in which people operate; and the other, professional. And after that, it's a matter of looking for jobs, and there women are exactly the same as men. To get a job you always have to find an employer who has an opening and it's that simple. There are no

154 career guidance and advice

secrets to finding them. . . . The best area to look always is the smaller station in the smaller cities, for two reasons: one is there's more likely to be an opening for the inexperienced staff, and the second reason is because it is smaller. When you first get your first job, you'll be doing many more things than a specialist does at the network level. Therefore, you get a very fast professional education, a technical education in the first three months of employment. And after that it's a matter of learn your job on the smaller station and go to a little bit larger one and eventually you'll hit the top. It's the way just everyone gets into the job of television reporter.

Av Westin offers similar advice to would-be reporters:

They should go to local stations, where they can become street reporters. There is no better experience now than to go out to a local affiliate and work the street as a street reporter and learn it, learn it, learn it. And then move up. Local stations employ more women than the networks. It's just a question of time before the networks will employ as many women as they employ men.

The emphasis remains on the need of the aspirant to acquire the skills necessary for proficiency in the field. Al Primo stresses the need to learn the basics:

One of the first things that one has to do is get the basic skills down. I think that it's like learning to drive a car. It's the hardest thing in the world for about a half an hour or two hours. . . . It takes all of your time and all of your concentration just to operate the vehicle. And if you devote the time to learning how to run the machine, then it becomes second nature. Then, you can really bring out your potential to contribute. But we have still, in this business today, a great many people who are still learning how to drive the car. And they spend all their day just learning. The mechanics have absolutely defeated some of the greatest people in this business.

Walter Cronkite believes that high standards are necessary for news personnel:

It is essential that news broadcasters be reporters first. Everything else in electronic journalism should be built on this base: a solid belief in—and ambition to be—a newsman, not a disc jockey, not a soap salesman, although both of these can be honorable and lucrative professions. . . . Ours is a postgraduate business. I think a youngster who wants to be a television reporter will eventually make a better television reporter if he spends some years in the vastly less complicated atmosphere of a newspaper or a wire-service room where the story—the whole story—is the thing; where he might spend a full day camped outside the mayor's door, and come up with nothing but frustration to show for his labors; where he chases fire engines, covers local courtrooms and government agencies; where he develops the persistence and acuteness to find the jugular of a story. It's an attitude he is seeking to achieve. And when he has developed it, we'll probably do the unkind thing: hire him away from the shop where he learned this most valuable lesson.[2]

2 Walter Cronkite, "Television and the News," in Robert Lewis Shayon, ed., *The Eighth Art: Twenty-three Views of Television Today* (New York: Holt, Rinehart, and Winston, 1962), p. 238.

Ted Kavenau feels that wire-service or newspaper experience is excellent preparation, especially for a woman:

> Go to a newspaper or Associated Press. The other day a girl came in here, a beautiful girl from Columbia and I looked at her and she asked me for a job and I told her, "Now look, I may have a job, but number one, you're too pretty. You'll be a disruptive factor in the newsroom. . . . And because you have this background, you have Columbia Journalism School and you have these really sensational good looks, you're going to get a job without fail." . . . She had an offer to go to Associated Press as a city reporter and I said, "Do yourself a favor. No one is going to take you very seriously in this business. Go to AP and get yourself some hard experience. . . . When you walk in after spending a year at AP, they're going to have some respect for you. . . . Don't come here," I said, "I would hire you for all the wrong reasons." I said, "Go to AP and get yourself a year's worth of experience and then go to a network and trade on your good looks. . . . Learn your trade; otherwise they're going to despise you and they're going to look at you as just another girl."

Al Ittleson has these words of advice for the woman who plans for a career in television news:

> Be ready to fight. Be ready for a little bit of a process of reeducation. . . . But don't come in so sensitive to it that when people see you they realize that your whole purpose is to prove a point. I hire people to do a job. If they can do the job, I don't give a damn what they are. Up until recently we weren't sensitive enough to realize that women were able to do the

same job that men can do. I've even heard the excuse that, well, a man has to support a family. Why
give that job to a woman who doesn't have a family
to support? It's ridiculous. That means a bachelor
shouldn't get a job over a married man. The only
thing a woman has to do is to really learn the business. Not come in as a woman and say, "I'm a
woman, teach me," because that's going to pass in a
year or so. . . . . The easier opportunity for women
that now exists, will not exist. So she'd better know
her business. She has to be a good journalist. She
has to be a rounded person and she has to realize
that in television, at least for the time being, appearance does count, personality does count. The news
is important but if no one is willing to sit through and
watch you because you're so God damned serious
about it, or so God damned intent on your point of
view, well then, whatever you say is not going to be
heard by enough people to make a dent. And, I think,
what you should do is learn the tools of the trade and
learn how to use them most effectively. And that's
not always as cut and dried as getting an A in journalism.

A network news executive proposes these guidelines:

Start at a relatively small station where they can
get a well-rounded background before they try the
top markets. Learn their profession and spend two or
three years until they really think they're good and
then come knocking on the doors of the New York or
Chicago or Los Angeles television stations. Don't in-
sult yourself if you happen to be attractive by going
there and thinking that you can be a pretty face and
get in New York television. . . . Because we're going

to hire on what we see in terms of a reporter. There
are reporters in the New York market who are terrible
and they shouldn't be on the air. And I think that
some of the reasons that they are terrible is that
someone consciously said, "We're going to hire an
Italian woman" or "We're going to hire a black
woman." Those things still do exist. When we all get
around to the point where we say, "Yes, we would
like a woman for this job, but she must be a sound
journalist," I think then everybody will be happy.

The chance of entering the television news world in a major
station in a major market with little training and experience is
slim but not impossible. Such "overnight" success remains an
added lure of the profession and an unspoken dream in the
hearts of many men and women alike. Kenneth MacQueen explains:

It can be done and it has been done, because in
the talent field, the abilities to communicate are to a
degree so rare—or you can visualize instantly the
superior—that it is not inconceivable that someone
who happens to be in Terre Haute, Indiana, can be
discovered and be so good they can come from
Terre Haute, Indiana, to New York City and be almost, if developed right, almost a star. So it's always
possible. . . . Talent in news, to me, is a lot like athletics, professional athletics. And while there are systems of so-called training and development . . . we
all know outstanding examples where somebody
. . . because of their tremendous abilities, made it in
the so-called big time instantly. And talent can do
that.

For the majority of prospective newswomen who plan to
enter the broadcasting profession, the shortest route pre-

scribed by a news executive was offered anonymously: "I have a perfect three-year apprentice program for her. Spend a summer in summer stock. Get a job in a wire-service bureau in Butte, Montana, and come to the big city and knock on the doors."

Women meet resistance to membership in the broadcasting profession at the point of recruitment. Opportunities for aspirants in television, both men and women, are limited. Only those who are exceptionally qualified and possess strong determination and perseverance should plan for this career.

The acquisition of a basic liberal-arts education with an emphasis on writing skills provides a suitable background. A graduate degree is not a necessary prerequisite, although specialization can provide additional options later in the career. Communicating skills are of paramount importance, and these talents must also be developed and strengthened. The ability to project ideas in a pleasing manner is essential. The technical knowledge necessary in television news, especially the ability to work with film and with the editing process, is best developed on the job. Consequently, a small television station is the ideal learning ground.

It is my opinion that any kind of job to gain admission into the station provides a suitable start. If necessary, offer to begin as a volunteer worker without pay. This may be possible at a college-affiliated station or at one of the educational broadcasting outlets. From the inside, mobility and advancement are dependent upon the degree of competence shown and the availability of a position. Be ready for the inevitable stumbling blocks. Phyllis Haynes remembers her early days as a trainee: "It was a very hard time because people never forget that you were the same person who went out for coffee no matter what you do."

Anna Bond, WABC-TV correspondent, was originally hired by ABC as a secretary to do stenography and typing: "Looking back, I can still say that was a good way to start, but there are lots of people who started with me who are still secretaries." [3]

Betsy Aaron has strong reservations about starting out as a secretary. She began her own career in this way because, for a woman, there was no other alternative:

> There was no way to get a job if you didn't have sec-
> retarial skills, no way. I contend to this day, if you're
> a good secretary, you'll never advance. The *only* way
> to advance is to be a bad secretary because once a
> guy gets a hold of you and you are his right hand or
> left hand or brains, he is *never* going to let go. And
> no matter how much he likes you, he's just not going
> to help you. Other men in the organization will help
> you, but your boss won't. . . . It's nothing to do with
> male chauvinism or anything. They would hold on to
> a qualified male as jealously as a qualified female
> secretary.

Whatever your initial job, it is necessary to be insistent as well as capable in order to move up. Sylvia Chase states: "I think they're as willing to give the job to you as a man, but you've got to let them know you want it. And that's one thing that women aren't very good about."

Be prepared to spend long hours on the job, and be ready to request additional responsibility wherever the opportunity arises. Lin Bolin, NBC Vice-President of Daytime Programming, is one of the highest-ranking women in any network's management. After working for six months at NBC she learned that the position of Director of Daytime Programs would soon be available. So she walked in and asked for the job. She got it. Although this remains the exception rather than the rule, it is now true that all the television networks have a policy of posting current job openings. This enables staff members, at all

3 *Mademoiselle,* November 1974, p. 183.

levels, to be aware of existing opportunities within the station and to apply for one if suited. Rising within the individual broadcasting organization is rapidly becoming more feasible owing to the implementation of these affirmative action programs initiated under pressure from active women's groups. However, always allow yourself the mobility to move to a better position at a different station at any time. Accept the inevitable rejections, and work more diligently for the acceptance that will follow. Success will always prove more easily attainable for some than for others, but with a conscious commitment, sincere effort, and acquired competence, a satisfying career in television news broadcasting is possible.

Somewhere along the line of development we discover what we really are and then we make our real decision for which we are responsible. Make that decision primarily for yourself because you can never really live anyone else's life, not even your child's. The influence you exert is through your own life and what you become yourself.

Eleanor Roosevelt

8
conclusions
and
implications

Women working in television news today are young, well-educated, articulate and photogenic. A close look at our 30 on-air television newswomen reveals a composite picture of a 34-year-old single woman, born in the northeastern part of the United States. She is the youngest child of a Protestant family in which her father is a businessman (salaried or managerial) and her mother works occasionally for economic reasons rather than for personal fulfillment. She is the first and only member of her family to enter the television field.

Our composite female is a college graduate with a liberal-arts major, and she has come to New York, the number one television market, through job transfer or advancement. Television was not her first job; she began her professional life teaching or writing for a newspaper or magazine. When she began to work in television, her first job was as a secretary, researcher, or production assistant. She got her job in television at a time when the station was attempting to increase the number of women on its staff.

Our composite newswoman is a general-assignment reporter for a local New York station and earns between $21,000 and $30,000 annually. She works between twelve and fourteen hours a day and often on weekends. She covers all kinds of news stories but finds herself often assigned "soft" news features. The demands of her profession leave her little time for any personal life. She has made a conscious commitment to her career, and television news is the dominant factor in her life. Marriage remains a possibility somewhere off in the future. She is bright, personable, and aggressive and works hard for recognition in the male-dominated news world.

This analysis of the "average" New York television newswoman suggests changes that have contributed to her acceptance and integration within the broadcasting profession. Her career path has been eased by the recruitment of other women, and her acceptance has been reinforced by legislation that makes discrimination against women in hiring unlawful. Because of the pressures of civil rights legislation and rulings of the FCC, there are very few television stations that dare not to have a woman on their staff. Women and minorities must be hired, so that at license renewal time, the station's management is not accused of practicing race or sex discrimination. However, it still remains difficult for her to participate and compete with newsmen at the same performance level. When stations have employed one or two women reporters, they feel that their quota is filled. A woman entering this profession must work exceptionally hard and do exceptionally well to be accepted seriously and not regarded as a "token" female.

The major portion of my interviews took place in 1973, in the midst of a general ferment in the hiring of on-air newswomen that was responsible for the largest visible influx of women in broadcasting history. This situation has stabilized over the last few years. Of the original 30 newswomen, 25 (83 percent) are now actively working in television and advancing their careers. Of the remaining 5, 2 were let go, 1 left because of illness, 1 remarried and moved away, and 1 reached retirement age. Three of these 5 women were replaced by other on-air newswomen. It appears, therefore, that although the original reasons for the increase of women in television news were pressure and legislation, their high retention value has resulted from the ability of most of these women to perform effectively under actual broadcasting conditions. Nevertheless, the overall number of positions filled by women has remained relatively constant. While few of these on-air newswomen have been replaced by men during the last several years, fewer men have lost their jobs to women.

Each of the women I interviewed, while acknowledging the more limited range of options available to women within the television news world, felt confident of her contribution to the broadcasting profession. Their thoughts and feelings are representative of women at a unique time in the growth of television news, but their efforts and experiences remain accurate testimony of the few who were able to speak for the many. Before granting permission to use their words for this book, many of the newswomen (and men) asked to review what they had said earlier, during the period of my research. All but two returned their original comments without editorial change. Elinor Guggenheimer wrote succinctly: "I haven't changed my mind at all in the intervening year." [1]

All the women broadcasting news today were hand-picked by men. This remains the common denominator that runs throughout the professional world, and reflects the current status of women in our society. Thus much of the difficulty cur-

1 Personal letter dated March 12, 1975.

rently experienced by women in assuming diversified roles in television has roots in the sex-role conditioning imposed upon both men and women in their daily lives. Marlene Sanders pointedly states: "The men we work for judge us by how they saw their mothers and by the kind of women their wives are," [2] and a prominent male news correspondent commented, after an assurance of anonymity: "A bright woman can do the same job as I do, if given the chance. But everyone plays their role—maybe the news director has a wife problem or the president of news has a girl-friend problem. His orders, therefore, reflect this."

Competence is the desired criterion, but hiring practices continue to reflect an emphasis on youth and attractiveness, so that the visual image becomes the basic asset for a newswoman. Reportorial and communication skills, prerequisites for winning the trust of the audience, must be built on this cosmetic base. Both the station and the viewers they serve seem more critical of women than of men.

The newswomen who have successfully maintained and matured in their respective on-air positions now find general acceptance and recognition within the established parameters of the broadcasting hierarchy, and the newswomen with the most seniority are recipients of added glory. In May 1975, Barbara Walters received two coveted awards for achievement as a television journalist. She received an Emmy as "outstanding hostess on a talk, service, or variety series." She was also selected as "broadcaster of the year" by the International Radio and Television Society, an honor previously bestowed on only three broadcast journalists—Chet Huntley, Walter Cronkite, and Lowell Thomas. The industry seems eager to reward a woman whose ability is proven and who is able to hold an audience.

Every woman working in the television news world is conscious of the transcience that permeates her profession, the

2 Quoted from the remarks delivered at Media Women's Association meeting, New York University, December 7, 1974.

need to fight continually to move ahead, and above all else the need to persevere in face of success or setback. A CBS news executive attributed progress of women in the industry to the competence and stamina of the pioneers:

> The few women who were in television news proved to be outstanding and I think they really paved the way in a way that we really can't appreciate. . . . Pauline Frederick at NBC—they were knocking down those old barriers about, she's not believable, she can't keep up, she can't do that and, by God, every time she came on she was keeping up. And I think people who have to compete against her would say, "You know, this is a good journalist. I don't see her as a woman. . . . She's a sound professional." And the executives and news organizations started hiring women, more of them. I think that trend was started long before NOW and before the recent women's lib. movement really sprang to the forefront. Although, I think, probably they have given some impetus.

While her work and achievements began long before the movement for equal opportunity for women became fashionable, Pauline Frederick's influence continues to be felt. In May 1975, she was the only woman in broadcasting named to the journalist's Hall Of Fame by the New York chapter of Sigma Delta Chi, "for her ability to make complex and controversial issues understandable."[3] It is ironic that the designation of 1975 as International Woman's Year by the United Nations came only when, after 22 years of broadcasting service to that organization, she was no longer its official on-air spokeswoman.

3 *New York Times,* May 2, 1975.

Women in television news today are helping to establish patterns that give expression to individual freedom and the right of free choice. Every newswoman works hard to minimize her liabilities and to maximize her assets. Television news provides an essential opportunity for both. Combining the tools of a journalist with the power of the television medium, the on-air newswoman knows herself to be a role model for others. Positive role models for women remain remarkably rare in television, a medium that generally creates and reinforces the classification of the female sex as secondary. The vast prime-time television audience repeatedly views women as "unliberated ding-a-lings, sex kittens, kooky housewives, lovable widows, crimefighters, secretaries and nosy nurses." [4] These "birdbrain roles" are reinforced over and again by the image of women on commercials. A study of the advertising seen in millions of homes during prime time concludes that women are most often seen as "decorative (sex objects) or useful (housewives or mothers), but hardly ever as professionals or working wives." [5]

When television does handle real issues and real people effectively, the results have impressive impact. In a review of the television documentary, "Three Women Alone," Cyclops wrote in the *New York Times:* "This was a visit to an archipelago of emotions that network TV has either systematically ignored or trivialized." [6] The personal strength and resources portrayed in Starr, a woman divorcee living alone, led this male critic to conclude, provocatively:

> Such discoveries in real life, are already intimidating men who need their women to be, in equal

4 Judy Klemesrud, "TV's Women Are Dingbats," *New York Times,* May 27, 1973, sec. 2, p. 15.

5 Joseph R. Dominick and Gail E. Rauch, "The Image of Women in Network TV Commercials," *Journal of Broadcasting,* 16 (Summer 1972), 259.

6 Cyclops, "Two TV Shows that Reflect the Changing Role of Women in Our Society," *New York Times,* June 16, 1974, sec. 2, p. 23.

measure, supportive and vulnerable. As you read this, bows all over this land are being tightened, and arrows are being fit to them, and somebody's pretensions are going to be punctured. Women alone, like Starr, can be lithe, sinewy, skillful, and not weep when trouble makes an obscene phone call. If those women have children, and the children are female, then they will percolate a revolution. About time, too.[7]

Progress in television, however, is made very slowly. Television news is continually concerned with capturing a large audience, and maximum profit remains the main criterion behind most management decisions. Since television itself reflects audience taste, which, in turn, is reflective of society, television will move only as society moves. The management of television is never in the vanguard of any movement. As Marlene Sanders declares:

I think that the women in the business and women in the society generally will have to keep up the pressure. If they make the small advances and then say, "O.K., we're going to be all right," they won't be, because people will slip back into their old patterns. . . . Women will progress in broadcasting as they do in every other facet of society.

Americans are beginning to live and to relate to one another in ways that are fundamentally different. The role of women in society is changing, and the changes deserve to be reported and reflected by the television medium in general and by television news in particular. A report issued in July 1975 by the Census Bureau indicates an increase in the number of women entering the work force, higher educational attainments by

7 Ibid.

women, and a growing economic independence of women from their husbands.[8] The next few years will show an increasing effort by women to use the force of law to improve their status in our society. The men and women in television news must work together to give full expression to these basic trends and emerging issues, so that broadcast journalism can effectively enlighten and inform the public.

Television news not only provides a focal point for facts and problems facing society, it offers a unique opportunity for men and women to be seen working together as equals. The dynamics of their job situation helps to promote equality off camera as well as on. Mutual respect grows when you are able to view another professional working well within the rules and requirements of the medium. Ability is the truest equalizer when permitted to be operative. Once barriers are broken down in the professional world, better opportunities for women, however limited their range, ensue. The increasing prominence of women in television news should benefit female aspirants to other professions who are striving to gain equal recognition for equal capability.

When a woman achieves a position of respect and authority, she often accepts the responsibility of advancing the influence of other women in her field. Lucy Jarvis, Emmy-award-winning producer of NBC specials and documentaries, declares:

> I always hire women on my permanent staff. Five Jarvis units are all women. . . . Yes, I am a female chauvinist. When the numbers are even I will change. Given two people of equal talent, I will always hire a woman. I don't say when there is equality, because I feel I'm better than most men. . . . Modesty is not a flower that grows in my garden.[9]

8 *New York Times*, July 7, 1975, p. 36.

9 Quoted from remarks delivered at the All Women's Breakfast, Cornell University, June 9, 1973, on the occasion of Mrs. Jarvis' 35th college reunion.

Complete integration of women in broadcasting, however, is going to be an arduous fight. Few feel that sexual prejudice can be eliminated without pressure, and real political pressure must continue or inertia takes its place. Even with a forceful, concentrated effort over an extended period of time, the outcome remains uncertain. Melba Tolliver expresses her own doubts:

> Anything is possible but I don't think it's probable in the near future or in the future at all. It may happen, but I don't think so. I question whether or not organizations like NOW, for instance, will continue the sustained drive of employment of women in broadcasting. I also question whether some of them even know some of the directions to go in once they've gotten on-camera people. It's the same thing that's happened to blacks, because television is so visual. You see a couple of people on hosting a public affairs show or on as a general-assignment reporter. Boom, you think you've got the whole thing wrapped up. They're not the people who are really running things.

A glance around any television newsroom in New York today reveals that in spite of recent advances, broadcasting is still a white male bastion, and indications are that it will remain that way for a while. Some in management are not inclined to change it. Ted Kavenau frankly admits: "It would bother me if I was a woman. But I'm not a woman. I'm a man. If I'm on top, I don't concern myself that much with those below."

Generally, management is the last stronghold of male supremacy and the ultimate goal of women who seek full participation in the broadcasting profession. Access to powerful decision-making positions would be the logical result of present advances. This, however, is not the whole answer. Pat Collins explains:

> We've always said that getting women into management jobs would solve all the problems. I don't see where that would necessarily solve all the problems any more than getting a black into a management makes it easier on the blacks. I've seen some very competent blacks and some very competent women. I've seen some competent but not very sensitive blacks and some competent but not very sensitive women take management jobs. And they tend to become, in their fight to go up the corporate ladder, they tend to blend in with everybody else and seldom fight for the rights of the people they are supposedly there to represent. . . . A limited one-dimensional, egocentric female who is in this business for the power and the glory that she thinks it is, will make no more contribution than the men who are in it for the power and the glory. Hopefully, we have better people than that in this business and I know we do.

Full integration is also thought to be some distance away because women are not given the opportunity to anchor the big network evening news programs. On the local level, more flexibility is in evidence as women are sometimes assigned co-anchor spots. However, only men are currently considered acceptable for the nationally viewed network anchor positions, the most prestigious in television news. William Sheehan defends this preference:

> You're really getting it down to too small a point at the top of the pyramid when you talk of the anchorman on a news program, the anchor person [10] on a news program. You know, there are only four in the whole world. There are Smith and Reasoner,

10 Our language, like the culture it reflects, is male oriented. There is, however, an increasing awareness of a need to use words that include women as well as men in their definition.

Cronkite and Chancellor. And it's such a highly specialized thing that I can't tell you who the next one is.
. . . We probably have ten people that are qualified
by virtue of background and experience and so forth.
But they also have to have that kind of magic that
makes people trust them and so forth. And who
knows who has that?

Younger men who take command of the decision-making
positions in broadcasting are more receptive to employing
women than were their predecessors. Av Westin declares:

What we now see phasing out in management in
all the networks is the first wave of guys that came in
from newspapers and things like that. The people

Photo: Allen Green/Visual Departures.

Pat Collins, WCBS-TV, "The Pat Collins Show," with guest
Martha Mitchell.

> who are right behind them tend to be more broad-
> cast originated. . . . So when they move up, they will
> be more tolerant of moving women up as well. . . . If
> you assume that management turns over every ten
> years . . . if we have a group that's retiring now at
> the age of sixty-two to sixty-five, and that's true at all
> three networks, the next group up are the guys who
> are somewhere in their forties. . . . That'll be ten
> years in which they will be more tolerant. Behind
> them will be another group. So I bet you within a de-
> cade there'll be absolutely no reason why manage-
> ment itself would be reluctant, even if there wasn't,
> as there is, an organized awareness that women
> should be moved along.

The passage of time and social change may yet make possible the equal participation of women in television news. Pa-
tience, pressure, effort, and excellence are required, now as
before. Al Ittleson advises:

> The majority of people are content with the way
> things are. What they have to do is fight the fight for
> themselves and maybe some of the residue will pro-
> duce a more equitable situation. I don't think women
> have it bad in this world. I just think if they want to be
> whatever they want to be, they should be able to be
> it. . . . There's only one thing that should stop you
> and that's yourself and whether or not you can do it.
> I don't think anything should help you either.

Despite the limited numbers of women in the field, and despite the real problems hampering further advances, opportunity for women in broadcasting, in principle, has become a reality. There are now few jobs in television that a woman is not
doing. As Betsy Aaron declares: "If you are an ambitious, quali-

fied woman, you can do anything in this business, but you have to be willing to make the sacrifice, and this is a brutal business for a woman." Ideally, ability will be the arbiter of success, and a reporter will be evaluated only as a reporter. Special consideration should not be given a woman, nor should special barriers exist for her.

It has been said that broadcast journalism must dedicate itself "to the discovery and communication of truth and to the improvement of the human lot. Anything less . . . is not just inadequate, but immoral." [11] If the television medium is to report with wisdom and understanding, it must reflect a range of images representative of all Americans. Only through the inclusion of competent women in ample numbers in the ranks of television management, programming, production, and reporting can the news of the world effectively present the aggregate view. As the television medium integrates its work force and thus becomes enriched by cultural diversity, it can project more of the total world. National television requires nothing less.

The continued quality of American life is dependent upon an informed citizenry, and only half that citizenry is male. A joint world in which the world of women is not separate from the world of men must therefore become the operative model for the broadcasting profession. As television news continues to recognize women as an indispensable resource, it can fulfill its responsibility to the people it serves and come closer to realizing its full potential. With excellence as a bastion, without sex as a barrier, women and television news will achieve their common goals.

11 Marvin Barrett, ed., *Survey of Broadcast Journalism 1968–1969* (New York: Grosset and Dunlap, 1969), p. 5.

interviews

Aaron, Betsy. ABC-TV. May 4, 1973.

Bell, Rebecca. NBC-TV (Chicago). May 16, 1973.
Borgen, Chris. WCBS-TV. May 1, 1973.
Brown, Theresa. WPIX-TV. April 3, 1973.
Bunyan, Maureen. WCBS-TV. February 21, 1973.

Chase, Sylvia. CBS-TV. February 21, 1973.
Chung, Connie. CBS-TV (Washington, D.C.). April 9, 1973.
Collins, Pat. WNBC-TV. February 20, 1973.
Corporan, John. WPIX-TV. April 6, 1973.
Cott, Sue. WCBS-TV. February 27, 1973.

Frank, Reuven. NBC-TV. March 15, 1973.
Frederick, Pauline. NBC-TV. February 20, 1973.

Grimsby, Roger. WABC-TV. April 23, 1973.

Guggenheimer, Elinor. WOR-TV. March 1, 1973.

Hanna, Lee. NBC-TV. March 8, 1973.
Haynes, Phyllis. WOR-TV. April 11, 1973.

Ittleson, Al. WABC-TV. February 23, 1973.

Jenkins, Carol. WNBC-TV. February 20, 1973.

Kavenau, Ted. WNEW-TV. March 5, 1973.

Lape, Robert. WABC-TV. April 4, 1973.
Lindstrom, Pia. WNBC-TV. February 1, 1973.

Mackin, Catherine. NBC-TV (Washington, D.C.). March 12, 1973.
McLaughlin, Marya. CBS-TV (Washington, D.C.). March 12, 1973.
MacQueen, Kenneth. WABC-TV. July 25, 1973.
McPhillips, Mary Helen. WOR-TV. March 1, 1973.
Margolies, Marjorie. WNBC-TV. March 15, 1973.
Marmor, Helen. NBC-TV. March 15, 1973.
Medina, Ann. ABC-TV. May 4, 1973.
Mulholland, Robert. NBC-TV. February 28, 1973.

Neil, Mike. WOR-TV. March 1, 1973.

Opotowsky, Stan. ABC-TV. February 23, 1973.

Pentz, Sara. WNEW-TV. January 26, 1973.
Pressman, Gabe. WNEW-TV. March 7, 1973.
Primo, Al. ABC-TV. February 26, 1973.

Quarles, Norma. WNBC-TV. January 23, 1973.
Quinn, Sally. CBS-TV. August 15, 1973.

Reilly, Trish. WCBS-TV. June 27, 1973.
Rivera, Geraldo. WABC-TV. April 23, 1973.
Rojas, Gloria. WNEW-TV. February 7, 1973.
Rollin, Betty. NBC-TV. January 31, 1973.

Sanders, Marlene. ABC-TV. January 24, 1973.
Scamardella, Rose Ann. WABC-TV. January 30, 1973.

Sheehan, William. ABC-TV. February 26, 1973.

Shen, Linda. WNBC-TV. February 28, 1973.

Sherr, Lynn. WCBS-TV. January 30, 1973.

Sherwood, Virginia. ABC-TV (Washington, D.C.). March 12, 1973.

Smith, Cabell. NBC-TV. March 15, 1973.

Stahl, Lesley. CBS-TV (Washington, D.C.). May 11, 1973.

Thomas, Judy. WOR-TV. March 1, 1973.

Tolliver, Melba. WABC-TV. January 24, 1973.

Ubell, Earl. WNBC-TV. February 22, 1973.

Walters, Barbara. NBC-TV. April 16, 1973.

Westin, Av. ABC-TV. February 23, 1973.

Zelman, Sam. CBS-TV. July 24, 1973.

bibliography

Allport, Gordon W. *The Nature of Prejudice.* Cambridge, Mass.: Addison-Wesley, 1954.

Bailyn, Lotte. "Notes on the Role of Choice in the Psychology of Professional Women," in Robert Jay Lifton, ed., *The Woman in America.* Boston: Beacon Press, 1967; pp. 236–45.

Barrett, Marvin G., ed. *Survey of Broadcast Journalism 1968–1969.* New York: Grossett and Dunlap, 1969.

———. *Survey of Broadcast Journalism 1970–1971.* New York: Grossett and Dunlap, 1971.

Barnouw, Erik. *The Image Empire: A History of Broadcasting in the United States from 1953.* New York: Oxford University Press, 1970.

Cronkite, Walter. "Television and the News," in Robert Lewis Shayon, ed., *The Eighth Art: Twenty-three Views of Television Today.* New York: Holt, Rinehart, and Winston, 1962; pp. 227–40.

Dexter, Lewis Anthony. *Elite and Specialized Interviewing.* Evanston, Ill.: Northwestern University Press, 1970.

Dominick, Joseph R., and Gail E. Rauch. "The Image of Women in Network TV Commercials," *Journal of Broadcasting,* 16 (Summer 1972), 259–65.

Efron, Edith. "What Is Happening to Blacks in Broadcasting?" *TV Guide,* August 19, 1972, pp. 20–25.

Epstein, Cynthia Fuchs. *Woman's Place: Options and Limits in Professional Careers.* Los Angeles: University of California Press, 1971.

———. "Women and Professional Careers: The Case of the Woman Lawyer." Unpublished Ph.D. dissertation, Columbia University, 1968.

Epstein, Edward Jay. *News from Nowhere: Television and the News.* New York: Random House, 1973.

Fang, Irving E., and Frank W. Gerval. "A Survey of Salaries and Hiring Preferences in Television News." *Journal of Broadcasting,* 15 (Fall 1971), 339–55.

Frank, Reuven. "An Anatomy of Television News," *Television Quarterly,* 9 (Winter 1970), 11–23.

Gornick, Vivian, and Barbara K. Moran, eds. *Women in Sexist Society: Studies in Power and Powerlessness.* New York: Basic Books, 1971.

Green, Maury. *Television News: Anatomy and Process.* Belmont, Calif.: Wadsworth, 1969.

Hole, Judith, and Ellen Levine. *Rebirth of Feminism.* New York: Quadrangle, 1971.

Jennings, Ralph M., and David A. Tillyer. *Television Station Em-*

ployment Practices: The Status of Minorities and Women. New York: Office of Communications, United Church of Christ, 1973.

Lipman-Blumen, Jean. "How Ideology Shapes Women's Lives," *Scientific American,* 226 (January 1972), 34–42.

Lyons, Louis M., ed. *Reporting the News.* Cambridge, Mass.: Belknap, Harvard University Press, 1965.

McLendon, Winzola, and Scottie Smith. *Don't Quote Me.* New York: Dutton, 1970.

MacNeil, Robert. *The People Machine: The Influence of Television on American Politics.* New York: Harper and Row, 1968.

Macrorie, Ken. "Objectivity and Responsibility in Newspaper Reporting." Unpublished Ph.D. dissertation, Columbia University, 1955.

Mannes, Marya. *But Will It Sell?* Philadelphia: Lippincott, 1964.

Mayer, Martin. *About Television.* New York: Harper and Row, 1972.

Mead, Margaret, and Francis B. Kaplan, eds. *American Women: The Report of the President's Commission on the Status of Women and Other Publications of the Commission.* New York: Scribner's, 1965.

Mencken, H. L. *A Mencken Christomathy.* New York: Knopf, 1949.

Minor, Dale. *The Information War.* New York: Harper and Row, 1972.

Murray, Joan. *The News.* New York: McGraw-Hill, 1968.

Mussen, Paul Henry, John Janeway Conger, and Jerome Kagan. *Child Development and Personality.* 2d ed. New York: Harper and Row, 1963.

Richardson, Stephen A., Barbara Snell Dohrenwend, and David Klein. *Interviewing: Its Forms and Functions.* New York: Basic Books, 1965.

Roper Organization. *What People Think of Television and Other Mass Media, 1959–1972.* New York: Television Information Office, 1973.

Shayon, Robert Lewis ed. *The Eighth Art: Twenty-Three Views of Television Today.* New York: Holt, Rinehart, and Winston, 1962.

Siller, Bob, Ted White, and Hal Terkel. *Television and Radio News.* New York: Macmillan, 1960.

Skornia, Harry J. *Television and the News: A Critical Appraisal.* Palo Alto, Calif.: Pacific Books, 1968.

Small, William. *To Kill a Messenger: Television News and the Real World.* New York: Hastings House, 1970.

Smith, Don C., and Kenneth Harwood. "Women in Broadcasting," *Journal of Broadcasting,* 15 (Fall 1966), 339–55.

Stone, Vernon A. *Careers in Broadcast News.* New York: Radio-Television News Directors Asociation, 1972.

Swallow, Norman. *Factual Television.* London: Focal Press, 1966.

Torre, Marie. *Don't Quote Me.* Garden City, N.Y.: Doubleday, 1965.

U.S. Department of Commerce, Bureau of The Census. *We the American Women.* Washington, D.C.: U.S. Government Printing Office, 1973.

Walters, Barbara. *How to Talk with Practically Anybody about Practically Anything.* Garden City, N.Y.: Doubleday, 1970.

Wood, William A. *Electronic Journalism.* New York: Columbia University Press, 1967.

index